View from a Long Chair

with an Introduction by Fiona MacCarthy

View from a Long Chair

the memoirs of Jack Pritchard

*For Rosmary from Jack Pritchard
1 May '89   with best wishes from Jack Pritchard*

Routledge & Kegan Paul
London, Boston, Melbourne and Henley

First published in 1984
by Routledge & Kegan Paul plc

14 Leicester Square, London WC2H 7PH, England

9 Park Street, Boston, Mass. 02108, USA

464 St Kilda Road, Melbourne,
Victoria 3004, Australia

Broadway House, Newtown Road,
Henley-on-Thames, Oxon RG9 1EN, England

Designed by Herbert & Mafalda Spencer
Set in Gill Sans
and printed in Great Britain
by BAS Printers Ltd, Over Wallop, Stockbridge, Hampshire

© Jack Pritchard 1984
Introduction © Fiona MacCarthy 1984

No part of this book may be reproduced in any form without permission from the publisher, except for the quotation of brief passages in criticism

Library of Congress Cataloging in Publication Data

Pritchard, Jack, 1899—
   View from a long chair.
   Bibliography: p.
   Includes index.
   1. Pritchard, Jack, 1899—   2. Architects—Great Britain—Biography.   I. Title.
   NA997.P8A2 1984   720′.92′4   [B]   83-22807

British Library CIP data available

ISBN 0-7102-0231-8

Frontispiece. Molly and Jack, in the Isokon Long Chair, in the flat at Lawn Road, Hampstead

CONTENTS

INTRODUCTION by Fiona MacCarthy — page 9

PREFACE — 24

EARLY LIFE
1. Childhood and schooldays — 27
2. The 1914–18 war and the Navy — 34
3. The end of the Navy, Cambridge — 37
4. More Cambridge and early jobs — 41
5. Henry Morris — 44

THE THIRTIES
6. Venesta — 53
7. PEP — 62
8. Children and education; Theta — 68
9. Lawn Road Flats — 78
10. Walter Gropius — 101
11. Marcel Breuer — 111
12. Moholy-Nagy — 121

WAR AND POSTWAR
13. Ministry of Information and Ministry of Supply — 129
14. Ministry of Fuel and Power — 133
15. Bratt Colbran — 140
16. The Russells, Herman Lebus and the design problem — 142
17. The Furniture Development Council — 150
18. GKN — 168

BLYTHBURGH
19. The Broads and the Martham Yard — 171
20. Blythburgh — 174
21. Final chapter — 178

SELECT BIBLIOGRAPHY — 185

INDEX — 187

Illustrations

1. Osbert Lancaster's view of Twentieth-Century Functional style
2. Clive Fleetwood Pritchard in 1884
3. Myself and Molly
4. The non-materialization of Sir Arthur Conan Doyle: scene in the Guildhall, Cambridge c.1920
5. Molly and friend at Cambridge
6. Myself, Fleetwood, Nancy and May about 1913
7. Cambridge to London and back by canoe
8. Myself as a young man
9. Henry Morris about 1938
10. Impington Village College
11. Entrance at Impington
12. Molly with Henry Morris in the early 1920s
13. Wells Coates in 1937
14. Sideboard designed by myself c.1930
15. Venesta stand at the Building Trades Exhibition, 1930
16. Later stands for Venesta
17. Alvar Aalto
18. Myself, P. Morton Shand and Aalto at the Paimio sanatorium
19. Molly with Jonathan and Jeremy in 1929
20. Beatrix Tudor Hart and Jennifer
21. Myself with Jeremy
22. With Molly, Jonathan and Jeremy
23. Walking with Molly and the boys
24. Beatrix with Molly, Jonathan, and Portia Holman
25. Jonathan and Jeremy with Molly in America
26. Molly in her mid-twenties
27. Isometric drawing of Lawn Road Flats
28. Early advertisement for Lawn Road Flats
29. Thelma Cazalet opening the Flats in 1934
30. Opening day at Lawn Road Flats
31. Lawn Road Flats: east side
32. No.6, Lawn Road Flats
33. Wells Coates's Minimum Flat
34. Standard kitchen
35. Standard dressing-room
36. No.15, Walter and Ise Gropius's flat
37. The Pritchards' flat
38. The Isobar designed by Marcel Breuer, 1935–6
39. Philip Harben fondue-making
40. A corner of the dining area in the Isobar
41. Molly with Harry Mansell on a tandem
42. Walter Gropius at the time he came to England
43. Breuer, and Ise and Walter Gropius: first birthday party for Lawn Road Flats
44. With Walter Gropius at Harvard
45. Moholy-Nagy's original advertisement for the Isokon Long Chair
46. The Long Chair designed by Marcel Breuer in 1936
47. The Isokon Dining Table designed by Breuer in 1936
48. Molly's consulting-room in Upper Harley Street
49. Isokon Dining Chair designed by Breuer
50. The Isokon Penguin Donkey Mark 1
51. The Isokon Pocket Bottleship
52. The Isokon Bottleship Mark 2
53. Prototype Square Table designed by Walter Gropius in 1936
54. Geoffrey Dunn, proprietor of Dunn's of Bromley
55. Egon Riss building the 'Isokon Line'
56. 'Breuer and Moholy-Nagy go to America': cartoon by Gordon Cullen, 1937
57. Harry Mansell and myself c.1940
58. Advertisement for the Isokon Penguin Donkey Mark 2
59. Moholy-Nagy in the mid-1930s
60. Delegates to the CIAM conference at Bridgwater in 1947
61. Minette de Silva and Le Corbusier at Bridgwater
62. On the Broads at Thurne in *Kay*
63. Mollie Thwaites, Edward Ardizzone, Russell Hoyle and myself on the Broads in *Twenty Six*. Drawing by Ardizzone
64–7. Our house at Blythburgh
68. Myself in a Long Chair
69. Simon Loftus at our fiftieth wedding anniversary
70. The Pritchards at Blythburgh

Note

In preparing my introduction I have found conversations with Paul Reilly (now Lord Reilly), one of the earliest Lawn Road tenants, and with the late Ise Gropius about her years in London particularly helpful. I should also mention the Pritchard Archive at Newcastle University as a major source of information. And, even more important, the Pritchards' conversations over many years of friendship.

I should like to acknowledge my debt to the 'Hampstead in the Thirties' exhibition organized by Michael Collins for Camden Arts Centre in 1975, which suggested several themes which I have since then followed up, and express my thanks for an enlightening set of notes entitled 'White Boxes for Intellectuals', originally compiled by Alan Powers for a Thirties Society Walk around Hampstead.

F.M.

INTRODUCTION

Jack Pritchard and the Hampstead of the Thirties
by Fiona MacCarthy

In the way that certain areas of great cities have an almost overpowering connection with past periods – Victorian South Kensington, the Left Bank in the Paris of the fifties – so Hampstead has become a kind of buzz-word for the thirties. It conjures up not only Hampstead Man and Hampstead Woman, leftish, argumentative, alarmingly progressive, but it also, in the popular imagination, evokes a blatantly uncompromising kind of building, of the style immortalized by Osbert Lancaster as 'Twentieth Century Functional'. Jack Pritchard will not, I think, resent the imputation – for Hampstead in a sense has always relished its own image of incorrigibility – that he and Lawn Road Flats, the block he built in Lawn Road, Hampstead, are as near as one can get to the popular conception of 1930s Hampstead. He (and they) were at the heart of iconoclastic Hampstead, the true champions of the modern as opposed to the 'moderne'.

Both he and his wife, Molly, coming from a fairly stolid middle-class professional background, had the touchingly courageous urge to think out life anew. To evolve a way of living by more rational principles. To plan out a style of life which was free and full and modern and entirely democratic. Although thirties modernists would scarcely have admitted it, this was in fact a pattern which had been quite long-established: it was after all the sons and daughters of these same quite prosperous professional and merchant classes who, with similar zeal and energy and comparable willpower in the overturning of the judgements of their parents, had been responsible for many of the great reforming movements of years past. Wasn't this the very place the Arts and Crafts Movement had sprung from? Although the 1930s modern idiom was very different, as Functional took over from the Country Cottage as the approved style of the artygentsia, and Dartington became the favoured school instead of Bedales, the motivation was not really so dissimilar. I like to see the Pritchards as part of a tradition which is really the old English middle-class tradition of service, besides being the epitome of 1930s progress. This is maybe something we should ponder as we read how Molly Pritchard, who had trained in medicine, switched her allegiance from biochemistry to work in psychotherapy, and how Jack Pritchard commissioned Le Corbusier to design a stand for Venesta at Olympia. At first sight such episodes seem almost clichés of that period. But looked at more closely, they acquire a sharper meaning as part of a whole pattern of English life and thought.

Jack Pritchard arrived in Hampstead via Cambridge. He had been at Pembroke, Molly had been at Girton, and the Cambridge contacts had always been important. It was certainly through Cambridge that Pritchard developed his ideas on the importance of relating art and science: again, a concept fashionable in 1930s Hampstead. It is also likely that his Cambridge friends intensified his sense that one should build for the period one lives in. The now rather misty but still amiable figure of Mansfield Forbes, the Cambridge don whose house 'Finella' was remodelled by McGrath, has become one of the legends of British early modern, and Jack Pritchard, who by this time was working for Venesta, had supplied 'Finella' with its experimental metal-plywood folding doors. Pritchard and Forbes shared a number of connections, not least with Henry Morris, great and controversial Chief Education Officer for Cambridgeshire, founder of the famous Village Colleges: the man who Maxwell Fry, who worked for him at Impington, described as one of the most delicious English eccentrics he had ever met. (One of his most endearing eccentricities was the suit in hunting pink which he ordered from his tailor for wearing in the evenings; but alas the brilliant pink proved too much for even Morris, and eventually he dyed it black and sober.) Pritchard was an undergraduate when he first met Henry Morris, and it was to be a life-long friendship.

On long Sunday morning walks, which were a Morris speciality, all tending to end up at some Cambridge village pub, Morris and his friends would embark on very vigorous attacks on the follies of society, especially the crassness of the current ruling classes, and this encouraged Pritchard in his taste for making plans to put the world to rights. Plans, programmes, memoranda, working parties, progress charts, statistics, were the order of the day. Statistics: the word almost became an incantation. Paul Reilly, who worked for Jack Pritchard at Venesta, remembers his office almost sky-high with statistics. Noel Carrington had a comparable view of Pritchard at the Design and Industries Association, of which he became chairman:

> If the early thirties were associated with the great depression they were also the era of the Plan. Our planner-in-chief at that time was Jack Pritchard – Venesta Pritchard, to distinguish him from his brother in advertising. The key to Pritchard's plan was concentration. All the resources of the Association, all its activities and propaganda, were to be concentrated on an agreed programme. Deviations, such as Peach's excursions to the countryside, would not be tolerated.[1]

What fixity of purpose, what immense self-discipline. The era of the Plan was almost made for Pritchard. Or did he in fact create it? One cannot quite be certain. There is no doubt of his founding role in PEP – 'Political and Economic Planning', to give it its full title, which was adopted in 1931. The name was his suggestion. He was extremely, even inordinately, active in the early years of PEP and was the chairman of the group known as Techplan (that perfect example of Hampstead thirties parlance) which was set up to formulate the National Plan of action. It was, poignantly enough, not a Shakespeare or a Bible which Jack Pritchard gave his sons when they set off to America in wartime but a copy of the Techplan *View on Planning* to sustain them through the uncertain years ahead.

In PEP circles the intense appreciation of the social changes which could be brought about by modern technology was balanced by a feeling of terrible frustration that the machinery of government was inadequate to cope with it. The outlook of the time is explained nicely by Max Nicholson in the PEP celebration volume *Fifty Years of Political and Economic Planning*: modern technology, it seemed, is rather useless 'if most of the invisible machinery to which this is connected is a Heath Robinson contrivance composed of the clutter of past generations and tied together with rotten bits of string'.[2] It was an attitude shared by the new architects. Maxwell Fry, for instance, a leading British modernist, was involved with PEP throughout the thirties. The national and indeed the international modern architectural groups and congresses which burgeoned in the thirties, producing manifestos with unfailing regularity (so many manifestos but rather fewer buildings), were unequally intensively rethinking basic principles. In 1933, the period at which the PEP Dartington weekends were in full swing, the CIAM group of architects was sailing through the Mediterranean discussing in great depth the problems of the functional city. This was a famous congress, attended by the stars of international modernism: Giedion, Van Eesteren, Le Corbusier, J.L.Sert and Walter Gropius. It resulted in the *Charte d'Athènes* (or Athens Charter), which was, to Wells Coates, the modern bible of town planning.

Wells Coates was the chief British delegate to CIAM. He was then, more or less, the leader of the British modernists. A few months earlier, he had formed the MARS Group (MARS for Modern Architectural Research), the small association of the more progressive architects and planners which was, in effect, the British modern movement. He was a member of Unit One, the collection of eleven artists and architects united in the strategic aim, expressed in Herbert Read's heady Hampstead phrases, 'to form a point in the forward thrust of modernism in architecture, painting and sculpture, and to harden this point in the fires of criticism and controversy'.[3] Almost needless to say, at the time of CIAM, Wells Coates was architect to the Pritchards, having worked on schemes for Lawn Road since 1929. Though the relationship had its squalls and dramas, the creative confluence of the ideals of its period made it a classic kind of partnership: rarely have architect and client been so well in tune.

This is what Wells Coates, just then, was feeling about buildings. The quotation is taken from *Unit One*, the book which the group of the same name published in 1934:

> What is the essential intention of the art of architecture? Reduced to its simplest elements, architecture is the art of providing *ordered shelter* for a multitude of human activities.... Every change in human conditions brings with it new possibilities of relationships of human needs, and the necessity to order them anew, to give them form, and freedom, and fullness and richness of life.... As creative architects we are concerned with a Future which must be *planned*, rather than a Past which must be patched up.[4]

Prospects of *ordered* shelter (note the italics) and *planned* futures; the underlying hopefulness for human progress; ideas that architecture should itself become the agent of change, opening up new possibilities for living rationally and freely – these were things in which both Wells Coates and the Pritchards believed deeply. And, as far as possible, Lawn Road Flats were to embody them. If the term were not so totally taboo in Wells Coates's circles, one could say that they were planning a shrine of modern living.

John Summerson has made the valuable point that hardly any of the leaders of the British modern movement were in fact home-grown. Interesting characters 'suddenly appeared', he writes, 'as if from nowhere'. They came from abroad, often from the Dominions, or had worked in 'something which was not quite architecture'.[5] Wells Coates was one of these, as were his friends McGrath and Serge Chermayeff. In fact he doubly qualifies for Summerson's description, having been born in Tokyo, brought up in Canada and British Columbia and having studied engineering. (He had also worked in Paris as a *Daily Express* journalist: he could well have been a character in Evelyn Waugh's *Scoop*.) Perhaps it was partly this disjointed early background, as well as an innate dramatic restlessness of character – as a young man, in a letter, he described himself as 'passionate, mystical, proud, inquisitive and fearless'[6] – which made him so scornful of tradition and convention and the whole settled bourgeois family existence. Wonderful Wells, who looked like Ronald Colman, speeding in his Lancia, breaking women's hearts: free untrammelled man, mythic figure of the thirties. A letter to Jack Pritchard, written in 1930, shows well Wells Coates's vision of ideal personal freedom, not to mention his effectively flamboyant prose style:

> this idea of property – so much of this little garden is for you m'dear and this tweeny little wishy bit is for me so there! – is *dead*, dead, dead.... My scheme provides a place which every actor in this drama can call his own place and further than that my idea of property does not go. This is the room where I sleep, this is where I work and this where I eat. That is the roof garden where everyone can turn out and enjoy the sun.... This is the garden where everyone goes. It's like a park. It's our little play ground and not so many legal acres to you and so many to me.[7]

Actually, Wells Coates had not designed a building at the time he met the Pritchards, a fact he concealed from his prospective clients. His experience up to then had been only in interiors: the Cresta factory and a succession of Cresta shops; the BBC Studios in Portland Place, which

Coates designed with Raymond McGrath and Serge Chermayeff; the remodelling of 1 Kensington Palace Gardens for Mr and Mrs George Strauss, in which, among the striking features of the main bedroom, were the double trays concealed beside the bed which, at the touch of a button, would spring out to form a breakfast table. These were seized upon by the architectural journalists as the ultimate example of Coatesian (or should one say Wellsian?) free life.

The scheme for Lawn Road, as it evolved slowly and often rather painfully, since finance from time to time seemed an insuperable problem, was up to then by far Wells Coates's most ambitious project. It had started as a house, but fairly early on, for reasons altogether obvious to anyone familiar with the ideology of thirties modernism, the decision had been taken that flats were more appropriate. Those were days in which 'larger' connoted 'freer'. The loyalty of radical architects was shifting from the old-time peasant housing, Arts and Crafts and Cottage culture, to mass housing for the workers, the massive flat developments which had risen up in Soviet Russia and Germany. In the pursuit of social justice and equality Lawn Road could surely not be anything but Lawn Road Flats. Nor could the flats be built in anything but concrete. The monolithic structure was almost certainly the first example of the use of reinforced concrete for a domestic building on this scale. The resulting building, so ideologically sound and architecturally, in its context, so amazing, was described by J.M.Richards, the architectural critic, as more like a 'machine à habiter' than any of the real-life buildings of Le Corbusier.[8]

The flats at Lawn Road were deliberately basic ones. They were designed specifically for young professional people, unhampered by possessions. They were service flats, with bed-making, shoe-cleaning and dusting provided for. Significantly, the flats had the most minuscule of kitchens, for tenants – as the original brief explained it – were expected to obtain their meals 'from a central source'. The Minimum Flat idea was the expression of Coates's own longing for perpetual mobility; it was a concept which he developed further after the war in his designs for Rooms-in-a-Frame, mobile houses linked to special structural frameworks which could even be transported to the country on a lorry and slid into a vacant frame for the weekend. The Minimum Flats were definitely meant for adults. The philosophy behind them, though not positively anti-family, postulated freedom from burdensome family commitments and a certain implied freedom from conventional morality. An interesting sidelight on the Lawn Road Flats development was Molly Pritchard's (non-permanent) liaison with the architect: this, said Jack, made working with Wells Coates, the prima donna of the British modern movement, that much easier. It was a brave attempt. When the Minimum Flat was reconstructed as part of the large 'Thirties' exhibition at the Hayward in 1979, its simple rationality, after all these years, was poignant. In its time and place, Lawn Road had been a pioneering work.

One has to remember that in 1934, when Lawn Road Flats were being finished, Hampstead still had a pervading air of old-time dowdiness. Paul Reilly, one of the original Lawn Road tenants, recalls it as the dullest and most bourgeois place on earth. There were just a few small signs, perceptible beginnings, of that tradition of avant-garde activity with which Hampstead has, over the years, become synonymous; the first glimmerings of that atmosphere of unrelenting open-mindedness and intellectual cut-and-thrust, the leftist-intellectual glory which was Hampstead in, say, 1937. When Lawn Road Flats were built, the Left Book Club had made inroads: a Hampstead branch was later opened in a Keats Grove house, the meetings of which, a survivor said, were 'vigorous'.[9] George Orwell was at work at Book Lovers' Corner, South End Green. The Everyman Cinema in Hampstead had just opened to regale the locals with programmes of films, many of them foreign, not generally available on the commercial circuits. The Everyman opened with René Clair's *Le Million*, and the films for 1934 included Flaherty's *Tabu*, Max Ophuls' *Liebelei, The Blue Light, The Blue Angel, Mädchen in Uniform*. The Everyman had a picture gallery, the Foyer, showing modern artists, mostly British, but some foreign. Indeed it gave Paul Klee his first British exhibition.

Among the Hampstead artists showing at the Foyer were Barbara Hepworth and Ben Nicholson, who had been living and working in Mall Studios, Parkhill Road, for several years. Although to begin with there was nothing formal or indeed intentional, about the Hampstead grouping – the 'gentle nest of artists' as Herbert Read described it – Mall Studios were then becoming the main focus for an important movement in painting and sculpture: 'The Continental British School', as it was later to be defined. Herbert Read, the art critic, and the main spokesman for the movement, lived at No. 3, Mall Studios. Henry Moore had a studio nearby, in Parkhill Road. Unit One, formed by Paul Nash, who also came to live in Hampstead, was a curiously typical Hampstead configuration: not just in its membership (Moore, Nicholson and Hepworth, as well as Wells Coates, were included in the original eleven); but also in its outlook, in its aim to do away with the old out-dated frontiers and bring about an integration of art and architecture. This was, at the time, a potent Hampstead notion, and it was the impulse which later led to *Circle*.

Artistic London then had a particular gregariousness, so very well recorded by Maxwell Fry, the architect, who comments in his memoirs that London was then much more of a living centre of the arts than it is now. Of London in the thirties, as of Paris rather earlier, it could be said that its culture depended on a couple of hundred people most of whom knew each other. He goes on:

> A few evenings later I was sitting in a studio in Hampstead – it might have been Henry Moore's or Ben Nicholson's, I cannot remember which. I was sitting in a window seat next to a small dynamic woman with a lovely rich voice telling her about my 'portal truss' as though

it were the gateway to Paradise; how one side balanced the other and the trusses repeated and were so simple and cheap to make and O, and O, if only, if only . . . (Then Ben came up saying 'Why don't you like my work, Max?' to which I replied 'But I do, Ben, I do. Only I am so busy on the same thing.') So little divided us then, the artists, the philosophers, the engineers, even the industrialists who were members of this society, drawing together in difficult days when Welsh miners sang their lamenting songs for bread along the gutters of Victoria Street and Ramsay MacDonald failed finally to charm.[10]

The gregariousness came from the artistic endeavour, the sense of breaking into whole new areas of experiment, and also from the youthful feeling of elation at being united in the leftist cause.

Max Fry captures so precisely the feeling of that period: the serious idealism mingled with a certain sense of amiable loucheness. Strong on ideology, yet tolerant and not afraid of seeming flippant at a time when 'gay' meant 'gaiety', no more. This was the hopeful ambience in which Lawn Road Flats were opened. The opening ceremony, by some process of selection which seems ideologically a little suspect, was performed by Thelma Cazalet, later Mrs Cazalet-Keir, Conservative MP, who broke a bottle. The first (temporary) tenant to sleep at Lawn Road Flats was Philip Sargent Florence, the American-born professor, economist and social scientist and national planner, art connoisseur, design aficionado, the man who two years later was to send Nikolaus Pevsner, a refugee from Nazi Germany, out on his huge survey of Industrial Art in Britain. (The survey was commissioned by Philip Sargent Florence's department at Birmingham University.) Man of science and man of art, crosser of international frontiers, public servant, bon viveur: Sargent Florence's combined credentials were remarkable. He fills the bill exactly of a Lawn Road ideal tenant, setting a high standard for the flat-dwellers to come.

A pattern of residency soon began to emerge. These were the main categories, as listed in a post-war Lawn Road brochure: Authors, Politics and Economics, Artists. There were enough Archaeologists and Egyptologists to merit their own heading. Though there were certain standard attributes discernible in the architects and writers, politicians and civil servants, mainly leftish, which Lawn Road attracted – modern men for modern flats – there were also always the misfits, the surprises, and this was one of the community's great charms. One of the least expected of the very early residents was Adrian Stokes, the art critic and painter, whose first major book, *The Quattro Cento: A different conception of the Italian Renaissance,* had recently been published. Stokes's artistic background, and indeed his whole conception of the civilized existence, was a long way from Wells Coates's, and, as the catalogue to his Arts Council retrospective so succinctly put it, Lawn Road Flats were 'the antithesis of his architectural values at that time'.[11]

From the start, Lawn Road became a cosmopolitan community.

Hampstead, with its artistic leanings and left-wing sympathies, was an obvious port of call for the numerous artistic refugees, the painters, sculptors, architects and designers, who fled from Nazi Europe in the thirties: quite a number of the members of the Artists' International Association, founded in 1934 and standing for the unity of artists against Fascism, were the well-known Hampstead faces. For the refugees arriving in London from the Continent, Lawn Road Flats were, in particular, almost a home from home, seeming indeed in many ways much more familiar to those from the artistic communities of Europe than they did even to the enlightened citizens of Hampstead. There was, first of all, the considerable tradition on the Continent, much more so than in England, of flat-dwelling for the professional classes as well as for the working population. There was also the idea of common purpose and endeavour between artists, architects, industrialists, scientists, the principles of artistic integration disseminated through Europe from the Bauhaus: ideas which were current enough in Lawn Road circles, though not, it must be said, exactly popular outside them. There was also the building. The Wells Coates Lawn Road idiom was very much less startling to the Continental modernists, to those who knew — and even more to those who built — the Weissenhof, than to the so-called progressive architects in Britain. For instance, Ernö Goldfinger, a Hungarian-born architect who had been practising in Paris, came to England in 1933 and found only two buildings which excited him: the Tecton Gorilla House and Wells Coates's flats in Hampstead. Lawn Road Flats were of the style which he admired and understood.

When, in 1934, Walter Gropius arrived in England it was Lawn Road Flats he made for. Or rather, it was to Lawn Road that the Pritchards brought him. The occasion was so momentous that Jack Pritchard remembers precisely the time of his arrival: it was 3.20 p.m. on Thursday 18 October. So deeply is Gropius's tenancy embedded into the mythology of Lawn Road in the thirties that it is in a way surprising to discover that Jack Pritchard scarcely knew him at the time he came to England: he had visited the Bauhaus but Gropius had by then left it. Nor did he even realize that Gropius had married for the second time and was bringing his wife, Ise. (Not that it mattered, for the second Mrs Gropius, as quickly became obvious, was *formidable* as well as quite formidable: just the sort of woman that Lawn Road Flats were built for.) The Gropiuses took to Lawn Road life immediately. Some time later, in a wonderful example of Gropespeak, the curiously formal Continental style of writing one often comes across in those Bauhaus-exile years, Walter Gropius expressed heartfelt appreciation of his interlude in Hampstead:

> For an observing architect from abroad this building became an exciting housing laboratory, both socially and technically, its positive qualities far exceeding its few shortcomings.[12]

Gropius lived at Lawn Road flats from 1934 until 1937, when he departed for America. Marcel Breuer, who had been at the Bauhaus through the twenties before setting up his practice in Berlin, came to live at Lawn Road too, a year after Gropius, and he too left for Harvard in 1937. Laszlo Moholy-Nagy, another Bauhaus maestro, also lived at Lawn Road briefly before settling at 7 Farm Walk, Golders Green (a peculiarly run-of-the-mill setting for Moholy), leaving England for Chicago two years later. Other Continental architect-designers were to follow: Arthur Korn, Jacques and Jacqueline Groag, Naum Slutsky, Egon Riss. Paul Reilly remembers his astonishment at finding Egon Riss, once a Viennese architect of great importance, offering, at Lawn Road Flats, to take his shoes away and clean them. This was Riss in a new guise of Hampstead intellectual valet. For Jack Pritchard did his best to provide the refugees not only with a bed but also with employment, a task which at that time required tremendous ingenuity. In his pursuit of suitable commissions for Gropius he once even took Lutyens out for luncheon at the Savile Club, an action, in its context, of remarkable self-sacrifice. No wonder that he earned the refugees' undying gratitude.

Procuring work for the distinguished refugees on a par with their status and their talents was anything but easy. The climate of the times was almost totally against it, and in spite of the efforts of Pritchard and others the evidence of those English years is sparse. But there was always Impington, the Cambridge Village College which Gropius and Maxwell Fry designed, which was the direct result of Pritchard's introduction of Gropius to Henry Morris. (The result was *orgasm*, says Pritchard: the image is unmistakably a thirties one.) Impington, though many critics have found it disappointingly self-effacing, was especially important in the standard which it set for British post-war educational architecture.

Jack Pritchard created several jobs for refugees in his own company, the newly formed Isokon Furniture Company. Gropius became the Controller of Design; Marcel Breuer was appointed Chief Designer. The classic Long Chair in plywood was designed by him for Isokon. Breuer was also asked to design the Isobar, a commission which in its way was just as memorable. The Isobar, which opened in 1937, was designed to be a kind of focal point, a social centre, within the Lawn Road building (giving it the edge over the modern block of flats which was in some ways Lawn Road's rival: Lubetkin's Highgate Highpoint). The Isobar was run as an independent club, drawing its members from the environs outside as well as from the Lawn Road tenants. It was a huge success from the outset, with a membership list of peculiar distinction. Edward Carter, for instance, wrote later, with nostalgia, 'Here for a while a bright glimmer of clubbishness shone in the Isobar of the Lawn Road Isokon flats.'

Evidently to begin with the Continental refugees found life in Hampstead baffling. Gropius complained that he kept meeting Conservatives who seemed much more like Socialists, so gentle were the nuances of the British way of life. The Isobar itself was a most esoteric set-up, linked to the 'Half Hundred', the Poor Man's Wine and Food Society which the Pritchards helped to found. Members were quite obviously relatively prosperous (though, confusingly, most claimed to be Socialist in outlook). They were, said Francis Meynell, a keen diner, 'word-wise' as well as 'food-wise'.[13] Besides Meynell, they included such literary gastronomes as Julian Huxley, Aldous's brother, the zoologist; Raymond Postgate, the radical-classic historian who founded *The Good Food Guide*; and Philip Harben, who later came to fame as the first television cook. The rules were very complex: for example every member had to cook, or at least plan, one of the monthly banquets, spending not more than five shillings per person on the food and five shillings on the wine; a two-shilling impoliteness fine would be exacted if any member failed to give advance notice of his non-attendance (Poor Man's punishment). The meals themselves would vary from the gourmet joke – one day it was 'the most disgusting menu that even a British hotelkeeper could conceive' – to extraordinary flights of expertise and fantasy. A London Zoo dinner, organized by Julian Huxley in 1938, included Bison's Tail.

The in-joke and the leg-pull, the intellectual gamesmanship – all this was very much a part of Isobar mentality. It sprang from the cult of non-professional nonchalance which so entranced Moholy when he arrived in England. He loved to think of England as the country of the amateur, pointing out with glee that almost all the leading English politicians – Churchill, Chamberlain and Baldwin – had had no administrative training whatsoever and that the Governor of the Bank of England was certainly no banker, a line of argument which went down very badly with the Headmaster of Eton when Moholy went to visit him. (He was not asked again.) The tradition of free thought, as Moholy-Nagy saw it, would have proved a safer topic in the more relaxed and cheerful enclaves of Lawn Road, where the spirit of the cultivated amateur was valued and where one of the main games was to ridicule pomposity. Were not the Flats themselves in a way a giant leg-pull, a flaunting of convention and respectability? There is, I think, a sense in which Lawn Road emerges as a feat of gamesmanship at its most English and inspired.

There was in the Isobar an obsession with weather, another quirk the foreigners were probably prepared for. The barograph, installed at the behest of Molly Pritchard and in honour of which the Isobar was named, was the dominant decorative feature of the Club Room, and readings were taken from it every day. British modernist architects liked the great outdoors. Wells Coates had a positive mania for sailing, and after the war he launched his own design for the Wingsail catamaran. Many of the famous modern buildings of the thirties in fact were seaside buildings: Wells Coates's own Embassy Court Flats at Hove, for instance; the Royal Corinthian Yacht Club, Burnham-on-Crouch, by Emberton; Chermayeff and Mendelsohn's De La Warr Pavilion at Bexhill-on-Sea. Nautical iconography is almost ever-present in modern British architecture of the pre-war period. At Lawn Road there is lots of it, a fact which was quite obvious to Agatha Christie, a tenant there in wartime: 'Coming up the street,' she wrote, 'the flats looked just like a giant liner which *ought* to have had a couple of funnels.'[14] The ocean-going image, with its overtones of glamour, very beautifully expresses the urge for exploration, the sense of possibility endemic in the period. Sailing with whom to where?

The Isobar members were also avid sunbathers. This was a further facet, I suppose, of new-found freedom; although if you look back you find that sunbathing (and windbathing) were favourite pursuits of much much earlier New Lifers. Maybe of every New Life movement since the world began. But the sun-cult in the thirties was especially remarkable in its influence on the new buildings of that decade. Thence Wells Coates's Sunspan Homes, first shown in 1934 at the Daily Mail Ideal Home Exhibition at Olympia; Max Fry's famous Sun House in Frognal Way in Hampstead; the Lawn Road Flats' sun terrace, very popular with residents. Thence too the caustic commentary from Osbert Lancaster on the fitness-for-purpose aims of thirties architects:

> new architects could seldom resist making a house fit for purposes such as sun-bathing, which the English climate and environment frequently rendered impossible of fulfilment.[15]

His accompanying illustration shows a Sun House and a couple of sun lovers. He wears a pair of shorts, she wears a thirties-style Bikini. This

1. Osbert Lancaster's view of the Twentieth-Century Functional style. From *Homes Sweet Homes*, published by John Murray in 1939

may have been the costume worn in less enlightened places. At Lawn Road Flats, however, you did not sunbathe in clothes.

Naturism. Sexuality. Progressive education. So many of the worst fears of the bourgeoisie were borne out by the preoccupations of the modernists in the middle thirties. There were obvious links between the new architects, with their determination to destroy 'the morphology of dead styles' (the phrase, of course, is Gropius's), and new educationalists. Wells Coates, when designing Hampden nursery school for Mr and Mrs George Strauss in Holland Park, made the very most of the space available – the ground floor of a large Victorian house – to encourage the children to express their natural feelings and develop their abilities unhampered. The design was strictly rational, from the long range of built-in cupboards to house educational toys to the retractable slide (extremely Wellsian); it was also inspiringly symbolic, with a large sliding-folding window to let in the air and sunshine of North Kensington. This was the pioneering age of nursery education – education carried out not by parents but by professionals – and a nursery school had in fact been included in early plans for the Lawn Road site. However, as Jack Pritchard explains with such disarming honesty, the worsening complexities of his relationship with Beatrix Tudor Hart, the prospective headmistress of the nursery school, gave him such misgivings that the school plans were abandoned. Such are the hidden factors which have always, presumably, helped to shape our architecture. It is an interesting postscript to the episode that, of Jack Pritchard's three children, Jennifer, his daughter by Beatrix Tudor Hart, was the one who eventually became an architect.

Beatrix Tudor Hart was one of the original teachers at Beacon Hill, the progressive school founded by Dora and Bertrand Russell. Beacon Hill was the school which the popular press of the day delineated fondly as the school where 'No Classes Are Held, No Punishment Inflicted and Clothes Are Barred in Warm Weather'. It was the school to which Jack and Molly Pritchard sent their boys, Jonathan and Jeremy, and Dora Russell, in her account of the school in *The Tamarisk Tree*, intimates that the Pritchards were almost model parents. She includes a picture of them watching a school play – one of those somewhat notorious school plays, exercises in democracy, written and performed solely by the children – with commendable expressions of unwandering attention. Dora Russell mentions that Jack gave the school 'a most useful long modern-style table with tubular legs'.[16] At one stage, she adds, Jack offered to collect his colleagues together to build a new school for her. One can well believe it. For Jack Pritchard's energy in disseminating modernism in the thirties was unbounded. Isokon furniture soon began appearing wherever progressive people gathered. Isokon tables in the Dora Russell dining-room. Preformed plywood bar stools in the Isobar in Hampstead. A Marcel Breuer table in Dr Molly Pritchard's very modernist consulting rooms in Harley Street which Christopher Nicholson, assisted by Hugh Casson, designed for her in 1938.

The art-and-science connection was an important facet of Isobar life. Molly Pritchard herself exemplified it perfectly. Julian Huxley is another good example. It was partly through his influence as Secretary of the Zoological Society that so many of the key modern buildings of the thirties were designed not for humans but for animals and birds. Indeed, Moholy-Nagy made a film commemorating *The New Architecture of the London Zoo*. Moholy, whose interest in natural phenomena also inspired a film called *The Life of the Lobster*, shot on the coast of Sussex, was, in his years in England, involved in a 'close circle', as his wife Sibyl described it: an art-and-science circle, Herbert Read, Henry Moore, Jack Pritchard, Julian Huxley, Barbara Hepworth, Ben Nicholson and Jim Crowther, the science correspondent of the *Manchester Guardian*.[17] J.D.Bernal, an expert in crystallography, and later Professor of Physics at Birkbeck, was also of that circle – which became the *Circle* circle – at a time when the relation of the natural and surreal was a great preoccupation both of scientists and of artists. Aspirations for command of the new technology were balanced by an unexpected refound fascination with ancient myth and magic. Related to this was the cult of *objets trouvés*. It was a mood recaptured very well by Myfanwy Piper in her article 'Back in the Thirties':

> There is a field at home where I always think of Moholy-Nagy, in his urban dress, with his bland and interested smile, holding up flints that he had picked up – little Arps and Henry Moores – incredulous at the sophisticated riches of nature.[18]

Fawley Bottom with Moholy. Itself a surreal scene.

Circle was published in 1937. This famous international survey of constructive art was edited by Ben Nicholson, Leslie Martin, the architect, and Naum Gabo, the Russian-born constructivist (an engineer and scientist by training), who had only very recently arrived in England. The survey was emphatically labelled 'constructive' as opposed to 'constructivist' because, such are the subtleties of 1930s usage, 'constructive' seemed a term rather broader, more embracing, more suited to a movement which aimed to represent not just a style of working but an attitude to life. Leslie Martin voiced the underlying belief of the contributors to *Circle* that art, whether painting, sculpture or architecture, can be one of the great constructive and unifying forces in our lives. Marcel Breuer, in an article on 'Architecture and Material', argued that it is not the new materials which matter so much as the new mentality which uses the materials appropriate to the task in hand. So rational and optimistic in its ideology, so solemnly enthusiastic in its tone of voice – *Circle* was a manifesto very much of its own period. Very much of its place, too, which was inevitably Hampstead. In fact most of its contributors – and also its reviewers – were Isobar members or at least Lawn Road habitués. In this context, Wells Coates appears a curious omission – an omission made good in the *Circle* exhibition held in 1982 at Kettle's Yard in Cambridge. In *Circle* retrospectives Wells Coates has to be included. For, as the organizers convincingly asserted, Wells Coates had been one of the foremost upholders of *Circle* philosophy in Britain at the time.

It sometimes seems that everybody one had ever heard of gravitated towards Hampstead in the thirties. Besides Gropius and Breuer and Moholy and Naum Gabo, there was Mesens, there was Mondrian and Meidner and Kokoschka and Fritz Feigl. There was also Sigmund Freud, whose son, Ernst L. Freud, the architect, designed a group of Viennese-North-London-modern houses in Frognal Close in Hampstead in 1937. Some of the new arrivals were more sociable than others, but, for the sociably inclined, it was inevitably Marcel Breuer's Isobar which drew them. Sibyl Moholy-Nagy, in her memoirs of her husband, writes ecstatically of the 'ever-open Lawn Road flats' and the endlessly generous companionship they offered: the stimulating ambience which the Moholy-Nagys discovered to be sadly lacking in Chicago. Indeed absent the world over. For the Isobar in Hampstead in its early years had a unique quality, inseparably related to that time and place and purpose. An atmosphere of serious intention, solemn subjects being bandied to and fro beneath the barograph. And at the same time a kind of quality of craziness, a sense of dislocation, broken accents, broken marriages. An irresponsibility engendered by the number of arrivals and departures, set against a background of political uncertainty. An atmosphere of highly charged emotional excitement epitomized, for me, by the reunion, as recounted by Jack Pritchard, of Naum Slutsky and Naum Gabo, two small men who shot across the Isobar to hug each other. They had not met since they left Russia.

Perhaps it was a process unnaturally accelerated by the war and the new ideas which succeeded it, but the special qualities of Lawn Road Flats became a legend very quickly. Nikolaus Pevsner, in 1955, was referring to the building as 'giant's work of the 1930's'.[19] In 1959, Sir John Summerson was giving it what is still its most convincing accolade to date, in his introduction to Trevor Dannatt's *Modern Architecture in Britain*:

> None of us, I suspect, would agree exactly which are the most memorable modern English buildings of the thirties and I must risk my personal choice. I will place first Wells Coates' Isokon flats in Lawn Road, Hampstead (1933–4) where both the client, J. Craven Pritchard, and the architect felt themselves to be the agency of a new force in English architecture and to be breaking the ice. Coates' axonometric drawing (which *The Listener*, unfamiliar with such representations, published upside-down) epitomizes the diagrammatic directness of this job and it is that directness which still arrests and convinces. This old dreadnought can still, in a way which, I find, very few of the early modern blocks can do.[20]

In the early post-war period, Lawn Road Flats won second prize in the Ugliest Building Competition organized by Cyril Connolly's *Horizon*. This too, perhaps, in its way, was no mean feat.

It was 1964, the year of the Bauhaus exhibition at the Academy, when I myself first saw Lawn Road. I was a young journalist working for the *Guardian*. Jack Pritchard had invited me to meet Herbert Bayer, the Bauhaus typographer then working in America, who had come over from Aspen for the exhibition opening. I knew nothing of Lawn Road; indeed, little of the Bauhaus. But sitting over dinner in the Isobar, as the exchange of thirties reminiscence heightened, I had a strange and moving sense of what it had once been.

Notes

1
Noel Carrington
Industrial Design in Britain
London: George Allen & Unwin, 1976

2
John Pinder (ed.)
Fifty Years of Political and Economic Planning: Looking Forward 1931–1981
London: Heinemann, 1981

3
Herbert Read
introduction to *Unit One: The Modern Movement in English Architecture, Painting and Sculpture*
London: Cassell, 1934

4
Ibid.

5
Sir John Summerson
introduction to *Modern Architecture in Britain* by Trevor Dannatt
London: Batsford, 1959

6
Wells Coates
letter to Marion Grove, 30 March 1926, quoted in *Wells Coates: A Monograph* by Sherban Contacuzino
London: Gordon Fraser, 1978

7
Wells Coates
letter to Jack Pritchard, 13 July 1930
from Pritchard Archive, University of Newcastle

8
J.M. Richards
obituary of Wells Coates in *Architectural Review*
December 1958

9
Edward Carter
survey of 'The Social/Architectural Background' in 'Hampstead in the Thirties' exhibition catalogue
London: Camden Arts Centre, 1974

10
Maxwell Fry
Autobiographical Sketches
London: Elek, 1975

11
Richard Read
biography in catalogue of 'Adrian Stokes' retrospective exhibition
London: Arts Council, 1982

12
Walter and Ise Gropius
quoted in Lawn Road Flats information leaflet
12 July 1955

13
Francis Meynell
My Lives
London: Bodley Head, 1971

14
Agatha Christie
quoted in Lawn Road Flats information leaflet
12 July 1955

15
Osbert Lancaster
Pillar to Post
London: John Murray, 1938

16
Dora Russell
The Tamarisk Tree, part 2: My School and the Years of War
London: Virago, 1980

17
Sibyl Moholy-Nagy
Moholy-Nagy: Experiment in Totality
New York: Harper & Brothers, 1950

18
Myfanwy Piper
'Back in the Thirties', *Art and Literature*, No. 7, Winter 1965
Lausanne: SELA, 1965

19
Nikolaus Pevsner
quotation from speech made at Lawn Road Flats 21st Birthday Party, 14 July 1955
Pritchard Archive

20
Summerson, *op. cit.*

PREFACE

Molly and I started writing what follows because of a dinner party in our house at Blythburgh. It was on Saturday 21 February 1976. Dining with us were Fiona and David Mellor from Sheffield and Bryan Llewelyn from London.

Fiona MacCarthy is a journalist who can record and report accurately, describing an event clearly and in a lively manner. She has written three or four books.

David started as a silversmith, became an industrial designer at the RCA and now manufactures and designs cutlery. It is a happy and apparently efficient factory. He also runs three shops, two in London and one in Manchester, selling a fine selection of useful kitchen equipment. David combines administrative ability with practical know-how.

I met Bryan when he was marketing manager for Greaves & Thomas, a fair-sized furniture firm. At the time of the dinner party he was a chairman of Thomson Travel and later became managing director of Thomson Publications.

Fiona, David and Bryan all said that Molly and I should write a book about our experiences and the people we have met. Rather an arrogant thing to do, I said, but they pointed out that it was no more arrogant than giving lectures, and I had given a few and had enjoyed doing so. Anyway, they thought we had something worth remembering. We said we would have a go.

Soon after the dinner party that started off this business I had the idea that Molly and I should write as a duet, each commenting on what the other had written. Such a book could be entertaining, providing we both had a high level of writing ability – which I certainly had not. When I sent my first chapter to Fiona, she sent it back. It will not do, try again.

The frontispiece picture of Molly and me in No. 32, Lawn Road Flats, confirms the rightness of Fiona's choice of title. It was from there that so much began to happen. The individual episodes may appear unrelated, but are they? Helping Morton Shand and Max Fry to release Walter and Ise Gropius from the degradation of Nazi Germany to live and work another day is surely similar to working with Max Nicholson and PEP to think anew about our own country.

There are many who want to stir up the *status quo* and search for a better way to go. That is the thread that I hope runs through much of my book.

Jack Pritchard

Acknowledgments

I have so many people to thank. I cannot type, which is just as well since my spelling is far from orthodox, so I must depend on those who can do both. At the start I must thank Mrs Challis, who could do both well, although, no doubt, she found me troublesome. I was then fortunate in finding Jane File; not only had she competence, she found my book of interest and gave constructive advice and help. When Jane's domestic load became too great I was fortunate in finding Barbara Rooke; she had the technical skills and also an interest. Then I had much help from Susan Thorpe here in the village. Without them I would have been in a great muddle.

Anthony Harris, a friend of our children, helped us in a different way. The book would have been far more verbose without his help – he is a remarkable word monger.

Finally I must thank Fiona MacCarthy. Without her there would have been no book, and throughout she has given wise advice and invaluable help.

EARLY LIFE

1
Childhood and schooldays

Since Molly and I have spent over half a century together we think we should start off by recording when we were born. I was born on 8 June 1899 at 6 Compayne Gardens, Hampstead, on the less fashionable side of Finchley Road.

My mother was Lilian Craven, from Keighley in Yorkshire. She used to claim that her great- (or perhaps great-great-) grandfather was a successful sheep stealer. She also claimed, without any foundation, that she was a direct descendant of the Earls of Craven; she had a lively imagination.

My mother had two sisters, Ida, the eldest and the most intelligent, and Nellie, pretty but somewhat stupid. Ida, the intelligent one of the three sisters, married Will Goldsworthy, a not very successful solicitor who wrote a book proving that Bacon wrote Shakespeare. Nellie married Richard Staward, who was a doctor with a practice in Nottingley, next to a canal along which steam tugs could be seen and heard towing a long row of many iron barges. They went clankety-clang.

My mother was blessed with a great deal of perspicacity. She married Clive Fleetwood Pritchard, an up-and-coming barrister, on 10 August 1893. My brother, Fleetwood Craven, was five years older than I and my twin sisters, May and Nancy, were four years older.

Sometimes my father would bring home a very large brown cardboard box of chocolates, de Bré, I think. On one occasion, he asked the twins which they would prefer – a box of chocolates or a baby brother. They both said without any hesitation, 'A box of chocolates.' Fleetwood is reported to have been very shocked. He was a very proper, upright elder brother.

We must have moved very soon after I was born, to 17 Maresfield Gardens, on the more upper-class side of Finchley Road. When my father died in 1914 my mother let the house to Belgian refugees. They put a large coke stove in the hall. My mother was horrified. But the Belgians understood how to keep a house warm. Our house had open coal fires in each room.

It was a fine house for parties – sometimes we would lay out yards and yards of a model train track from room to room on the top floor.

My grandfather was born on 8 September 1834, in the reign of William

2. Clive Fleetwood Pritchard, my father, in his rooms at Cambridge in 1884

IV. It was said that he had had tea with the great social reformer Robert Owen. He was a small man with mutton-chop whiskers and a twinkle in his eye. My grandmother, whose maiden name was Titford, was a colourless woman.

There is a story that Grandfather was offered a knighthood, which put him in a dilemma. Towards the end of the nineteenth century there was quite a significant republican movement, and as a republican he could not accept the honour. On the other hand, he was a constitutionalist, and so could not refuse it. He got out of his dilemma by insisting that they had got the wrong Pritchard, and going on insisting till they understood – or that was the story as I first heard it. In fact, he was offered the knighthood twice, the second time by his friend John Burns, who was then the President of the Local Government Board.

Later, when we were presenting our first-born to Grandfather, he asked Molly what we were going to call him. When she said Jonathan, he remarked, 'That'll sound good when he is Sir Jonathan Pritchard.'

Christmas lunch at my grandfather's was a solemn occasion. My aunts, Hilda and Bertha, would welcome us. We called them the Happy Little Aunts. Bertha was deaf, but Hilda was gay and great fun – and very worthy. On one occasion, when trying to persuade a recalcitrant father to go back to his wife and children, she stood outside a dirty public house – it would not be proper for her to go inside.

Between lunch and tea on Christmas Day the children would have to recite; but we knew there was a secret. The study door would be locked. Then, after tea, we would find the door unlocked. Inside, it was dark and smelt of candles, and there we would find Father Christmas. Father Christmas turned out to be my Uncle Wilfred, my father's youngest brother. He was not a great success in life, but he was excellent with children even though he never married.

My early schooldays at prep schools in Hampstead were on the whole not fortunate. At first I was sent to West Heath School, where I did not learn to read until I was eleven so was always considered a dunce. No one had yet heard of dyslexia – perhaps that was part of my trouble and not the supposed inefficient teaching at West Heath. All the same, I was reasonably happy.

I was then sent to Heath Mount, where I was not happy at all. Alec Waugh was there, and later in *The Loom of Youth* he described it as I would. It was disagreeable – very strict, with a martinet of a headmaster.

At about twelve or thirteen I followed Fleetwood to Oundle. I don't think there can have been such a thing as the 'Common Entrance' in those days. On the whole my years at Oundle were a success, largely owing to the influence of F.W.Sanderson, the headmaster, the first scientist to be headmaster of a public school. He encouraged us to form our own opinions, based on the facts.

I was reminded of this after I had left school and joined the Navy. Not long after the Russian Revolution when I was on leave, I went back to Oundle on a visit. I had welcomed the revolution at first, but at times I would swallow without thought what the popular press was saying – how immoral and wicked the Bolsheviks were. On this visit to Oundle I said to Sanderson that perhaps the Bolsheviks *were* very wicked. Sanderson just looked me straight in the eye and asked, 'What is wrong with the Bolsheviks?' Of course, I hadn't a clue. That started me thinking.

Some years later, during the General Strike, Molly and I were delivering the workers' papers. We called in at Oundle and sold a bundle to the local newsagent opposite School House. They knew me, of course, as a respectable Oundelian and therefore accepted the papers. Sanderson had died and the new head, Kenneth Fisher, saw the wicked workers' paper in the shop and demanded how it came to be on sale. His boys should not see such rubbish. Fisher then found us in the market place and gave us both a severe dressing-down.

I can imagine how Sanderson would have behaved. Courteous, and simply saying how interesting; only why were we doing it?

3. Myself and (*right*) Molly, both aged about fifteen

I sometimes wonder whether the headmasters of Oundle who have followed Sanderson have read and understood his philosophy.

Molly now tells her story:
My family was not unlike Jack's. My father was a solicitor, while Jack's was a barrister, but I think Jack's family had been middle-class longer than mine. I always understood that my great-grandfather was a plumber. My mother, Rose, was the fourth daughter of the senior partner in my father's firm.

My parents got married in Canada because an Act of Parliament, now rescinded, said that a man might not marry his deceased wife's sister. My father, Henry Cooke, had previously been married to one of my mother's elder sisters, who had died in childbirth.

We lived at 47 Streatham High Road. I was born on 8 January 1900, very convenient because there is only one week in the year when I am not the same age as the century. My sister, Jill, was two years older than I and my brother George was two and three-quarter years younger. When Jill and I were taken into my mother's bedroom to see the newborn baby I said, 'I wish it was a baby pony.' This did not last long, and George became my favourite person; but I often squabbled with and hit out at him. I was a very naughty and disagreeable child. I was named Rosemary because, when I was born, my mother thought I was a sweet little flower. By the time I was a year old I had disabused her of this idea, so she decided to cut it down to Molly (thank goodness).

Many years ago now, I thought of writing about my childhood, and would have called my account 'Black Sheep, Black Horse'. I was certainly the black sheep of the family, and all my fantasies were about being, or riding on, a beautiful prancing black steed.

This passion dates from a very early age. My mother said that when I was barely a year old I would scream when my pram was pushed into a side road because there were no horses to look at, whereas there were plenty on the main road. Jack told me that he used to go to school on a horse-drawn bus along Finchley Road. He always got on the top and sat as near as he could get to the driver. I used to do this too.

Jill and I went to a little nursery school in the corner house facing Tooting Common – I must have been three and a half or four. I enjoyed it there, but I don't think we stayed there very long, because I remember that before we left Streatham my mother found a splendid governess for us – Miss Herford. I have always had a warm spot for her in my heart because she gave us a book written by her brother, who lived in America. It was an illustrated alphabet, there were rhymes for each letter, and two of them I frequently quote:

> O is for optimist glad,
> Who doesn't know how to be sad.
> If he woke up one day,
> In Hades he'd say,
> 'Well, really, it isn't so bad.'

Attached there was a picture of him warming his hands by the blazing fiery furnace.

The other quotation I remember is:

> P is for pessimist gruff,
> Who often goes off in a huff.
> If he happened to gain
> Heaven's gate he'd complain
> Of his halo and harp, like enough.

And the picture shows a man in angel's costume standing in front of a mirror holding his halo over his head and looking very displeased at what he sees.

When I was seven we moved to Kensington and lived in one of a row of Georgian houses in Argyll Road. Miss Herford came with us and taught us for at least another year.

My father often strummed on the piano and played bits from Beethoven sonatas and Bach and Chopin. In his young days he wished to become a concert pianist. He and my mother used to play duets and my love of music started from those days. There was a time when I wished to be an opera singer, but my ear was too good for my voice. I could never produce the note I was thinking of.

There was music on my mother's side of the family too, and art. Her father and eldest sister, Lily, were both watercolour painters, and her sister Annie was a splendid violinist.

Though I do not remember my grandfather, I well remember my grandmother. She always wore black and, of course, ample long skirts. Her hair was white and was combed into a large roll across the front of her head. She sometimes wore a white lacy cap.

Auntie Lily, the painter, also did lovely embroideries and made a beautiful altar screen for the parish church at Haslemere. I remember it as being rather Art Nouveau in style. Many years later we taught her to drive a car, a Lea Francis. Annie, the violinist, organized a very good amateur orchestra at Haslemere. They gave weekly concerts and often got very well-known musicians to come and play with them or to conduct. She was also a very good actress and could take off her friends and acquaintances.

Another aunt had married a man named Lawford. We always called him Uncle Ben. He had a very good tenor voice so he always sang the hero's part in the Gilbert & Sullivan operas which my aunts and their friends got up every Easter holiday. We loved them.

How my parents achieved it I don't know, but I remember that we all had the greatest contempt for children who *wasted* their pocket money on *sweets*. We would save up for two or three weeks and then buy something really good, such as a box of tin soldiers (sixpence) or a bow (two shillings and sixpence) and arrow (sixpence). Not bad considering the pocket money we used to get in those days: a penny a week for each year of our age.

My grandmother had a carriage and a pony cart. The horse which pulled the carriage was a dark chestnut called Trojan, and the pony trap was pulled by Cocoa, a substantially built red-roan cob. Whenever possible I used to go riding on Cocoa, accompanied by Grandma's coachman on Trojan.

My favourite sports have always been those in which one is pitted against nature rather than against other people – tree-climbing, riding, an interlude of ice- or roller-skating, later rock-climbing and, still persisting even now, sailing.

My interest in sailing was early aroused by my father's stories about the time when, at fifteen or sixteen, he sailed to Australia in a square-rigger. I began sailing model yachts very early. So did Jack. I started with a little boat for which I had saved up my pocket money. Then one evening my father's friend Montague Napier (the designer of the then famous Napier cars and later of the Napier Lion aero engine), who had come to have dinner with my parents, came upstairs to kiss me good night; a sovereign, a real gold one, slid out of his pocket. I picked it up and said 'This will just do for that model yacht I want to buy.'

Of course I gave it back to him at once, but the next day his magnificent six-cylinder Napier car drew up at our front door carrying the most splendid and the largest model yacht I had ever seen. It was my greatest treasure. I used to wheel it to the Round Pond in my doll's pram – the only thing I ever used that pram for.

My father's family were not, so far as I know, attached to any church. I do not know if his father was also atheistically inclined, but my father was. In those days it was, of course, considered very indiscreet for professional men not to go to church. I was occasionally taken to see my aunts' work in their parish church at Haslemere, but I think I only went once to the church at Streatham and I can't remember why. (At boarding school, of course, one took it for granted and went along with all the others.)

When I was just nine my parents – wisely, I think – decided that I was too upsetting an influence in the family and that boarding school would be the answer. There was a delightful small girls' boarding school near Hindhead, only about four miles from our aunts' house at Haslemere.

The teaching was very good – at least, I thought so at the time. My favourite teacher of all was Miss Fuller, the science teacher. In the winter, if it was fine and not too cold, she would take us out in the evenings and point out the planets and the main constellations. I have never forgotten them, but most of all I remember her placing a prism in a ray of sunlight and showing us how the rainbow colours appeared on a sheet of white paper. After that day I was going to be a scientist; and to my mind, then, the peak of science was medicine. (It was well after I qualified that I came to the conclusion that, although some scientific background is essential, treating patients is an art rather than a science. I scarcely begin to understand modern science – atom smashing, lasers, quasars and all that.)

The school had good grounds, about five acres. What I liked were the trees. I would have liked to be able to boast that I had climbed them all, but there were many I did not achieve. We weren't allowed to get up before 6.30 a.m., but I always woke early, and when it was light enough I would hop out of bed at 6.30 sharp and rush out and climb trees until breakfast time. We had a scout group in the school and I was keen on that. We were scouts, not guides.

I left Lingholt when I was thirteen and went to the Godolphin and Latymer School. I think I quite liked it there, though I haven't any very vivid memories of it.

When the war broke out in 1914 we were spending our summer holiday in Aldeburgh. There my 'girl scout' experience from Lingholt came in useful. The local scoutmaster mustered several of the holiday youngsters into a team to 'guard the telephone wires going down to Orford Lighthouse'. We used to meet at the point where the river Alde comes closest to the sea (100 yards) before turning south and wandering down for sixteen miles before going into the sea. There we would be picked up by a small sailing boat, and we sailed down to a point near the lighthouse. One day the owner of the boat allowed me to take the tiller. I was naturally very delighted (and, I hope, acquitted myself well).

2
The 1914–18 war and the Navy

The narrative reverts to Jack:
The 1914 war came upon us very suddenly. Few believed it would really happen, and my father died without knowing much about it.

At school it had never crossed our minds that we might be defeated or come perilously near to it. Fleetwood was finishing his first year at Cambridge and immediately joined up in the Field Artillery; in those days a public school boy who had been in the OTC would almost automatically be assumed to be officer material.

At Oundle I remained in the bottom form but one until I was transferred to the Army class, which prepared boys for becoming officer cadets in the Army Engineers, the Marines and the Navy. The examinations for each service were very similar. My mother believed that I was not so clever as her eldest son and that I should try and get into a service that would give me a career for life.

I understood that there were vacancies for about thirty naval cadets, so I took the entrance examination. When the results came through I found that I had been accepted in spite of losing about 700 or 800 marks for bad spelling and bad handwriting and getting almost nil for French. The reason for my being chosen was not that I was so much better in the other subjects but that there had been great losses at sea and more cadets were needed. Even so I only just scraped through.

I reported to Keyham, Devonport, in the summer of 1917. Much of the teaching meant learning by rote rather than by reason, due no doubt to the need for rapid training and instant obedience. It did not suit the development of my questioning mind.

On joining my ship, HMS *Lion*, I was shown round by the senior midshipman, McKoy, a smart young man with his cap just at the right angle. He said how unfortunate it was that I had joined through Keyham and not through Osborne or Dartmouth. I soon understood the significance of that remark.

In the gun room, which is the mess for midshipmen and sub-lieutenants, the atmosphere was very different from what I had expected. It was rather like being back at prep school. Those of us from Keyham were older than the others, but we were junior to them. A year or so at that age is important, especially in a situation in which we older men would be expected to fag for the younger midshipmen. There was trouble to come.

In a letter to my mother, written four days after joining, I said, 'There is a most extraordinary state of affairs in the gun room.' Such juvenile behaviour on a battleship at war came as a great surprise to me. At the end of the letter I wrote, 'I suppose if the Keyham fellows wanted, we could put a stop to it, being in the majority.'

We did just that sooner than I expected. It was sparked off when the President of the Mess, a somewhat childish sub-lieutenant at that time, tried to put into practice an old tradition that junior midshipmen should be beaten up and chased round the ship. This seemed a pointless tradition to begin with. The signal that was intended to commence the exercise was the President sticking a fork into a beam – which was difficult in itself, since ships were no longer made of wood. We Keyham men refused to move.

No effort was made to drive us out. The President complained to the lieutenant commander responsible for midshipmen, who reported us to the Commander, who in his turn reported us to the Captain. At this point I was away for a few days with suspected mumps. When I returned I was told that the President of the mess had been reprimanded by Captain Backhouse, and in my diary I wrote: 'Our mutiny has been successful – the gun room is now a republic!' Many years later I met a full captain RN, and told him of our dreadful behaviour. At first he took it seriously, saying, 'You should have been for the high jump.' Then he asked when it had happened, and his next comment was very interesting. He told me that some months after our episode, he, on such and such a battle ship, began to be treated in a more adult manner.

An odd thing happened during those few months. I was won over by a smooth young High Anglican padre, who had me confirmed, although I had not been baptized. Previously the nearest approach to Christianity was being taken to the Unitarian chapel in Quex Road, Kilburn, and, of course, compulsory chapel at school. There I had learned what fun it was to take a bumble bee in a matchbox and set it free in the chapel. It was fascinating to see how long it was able to keep everyone's attention.

I found it strange that on a ship of war there was a padre preaching

Christianity. I wondered what Jesus would have thought. Years later I went to see the padre and was able to talk to him on more equal terms; what surprised me then was his almost passionate objection to Guild Socialism. I suggested that it might not be a bad idea to provide conditions where all in a firm could have some say in its management. He seemed to hate the idea without any basis of reason.

The Navy was an interesting experience for me. At times life seemed very ordinary, with long walks ashore and guests to dinner. Even when we were at sea, which was most of the time, the war often seemed far away. There were many busy and exciting times, when the war became a reality, but I was never certain how I would react in a serious battle. Would I have done my duty efficiently?

I particularly enjoyed being 'tanky', the navigator's assistant. It gave me an opportunity to think and question. Captain Jones, the navigator, combined logical thinking with a remarkable understanding for his job. He taught me a great deal. It was a new experience to be taught as an individual capable of making decisions.

During this time, when I had to spend some time in hospital, I met an American ensign – comparable with a midshipman. He later invited me to his ship. It happened to be on a day when we were to coal ship. This was traditionally done by all ranks in the Navy, but because the invitation was from a foreign ally, I was reluctantly given permission to be absent. Perhaps I should have proudly refused, saying that all ranks in the British Navy coaled ship, but I thought better of this. I was intrigued to find out what a US battleship was like. She was exceedingly clean, helped no doubt by being oil fuelled, but I was surprised in some ways that the US ships were not as mechanically efficient as we were. Those of all ranks on duty were very smart and disciplined, but easy off duty. This was different from the British Navy in those days, when the officers were officers, and the men, men. What was most noticeable was that the American ensigns were regarded and treated as adults, and not schoolboys, as we were.

The unconscious process that led to my decision to leave the Navy must have started in about October 1918, while midshipmen were working for their promotion exams. I found signals difficult, Morse seemed to dazzle me and my erratic and far from orthodox spelling did not make it any easier. I was examined by the Captain in his cabin. I knew I would have to read two messages flashed by a chief petty officer, and I found out what they were to be. Unfortunately he signalled them in the reverse order from what I had expected. The Captain roared with laughter.

Meanwhile, efforts to persuade the German Cabinet to sign the peace treaty were getting under way. I remember how proud I was that the Allies accepted President Wilson's fourteen points for the Germans to lay down their arms. Few in the gun room had expressed that view: most said we should do what we and the Allies ultimately did – the consequences of which we now know only too well.

We in the first British battle cruiser squadron escorted the German cruisers for internment in Scapa Flow. Beatty, the Commander-in-Chief, had been on board to speak to us about how to behave to the Germans. They should be treated with 'cold courtesy' but we must remember they were 'despicable beasts'. It seemed to me that this was hardly the sort of thing the Commander-in-Chief should say. He had continued: 'The British sailor is very sympathetic. We know that he has a very large heart, and sometimes a very short memory. In this case just contract your heart and lengthen your memory, and remember that the enemy you are looking after is despicable, nothing more nor less.' I could not understand why the Germans, as people, should be considered so different from ourselves. They had achieved much in literature, science and industry, and after all, they were a cultivated and civilized people just as we were.

When the Germans scuttled their ships in Scapa Flow, many in Britain threw up their hands in anger saying it was a dirty thing to do. I wondered why. It certainly reduced much bickering amongst the Allies over who should have what.

I had been in the Navy from 1917 until about the middle of 1919. I retired in sufficient time to study at the London Polytechnic in Regent Street, and then went on to Cambridge.

I had gone to sea about twenty times without getting very near to a naval action.

3
The end of the Navy, Cambridge

When I retired from the Navy, I took an aptitude test at the Pelman Institute. It suggested that engineering would be a suitable occupation for me, which would presumably mean something to do with industry. As I wanted to go to Cambridge I should try for the engineering tripos. Not being certain if I could afford more than two years, I went up for the Long Vac in the summer of 1920. On the very first weekend I was invited by a Southwold friend to join a party on the river. The party included undergraduates reading very different subjects. One was doing medicine. She and I seemed to know our feelings for each other from the start and, although we were to have other peccadilloes on the way, it was inevitable that Molly and I would ultimately come together.

My two years at Cambridge were a most important time for me, bringing colour and shape to so much of my life. Instead of the necessarily imposed discipline of the Navy, I could now do, think, reason why, and say what I liked and work out my own discipline. I worked hard, went to many lectures, some outside my subject, and also had a good time. It was like bright sunlight and an ever-expanding view.

When I decided to take economics as well as engineering, I found a series of lectures that were not on the list for either of my two chosen subjects but seemed to straddle both: 'The scope for industrial psychology' given by Philip Sargent Florence.

The course covered among other things method and time study, and vocational guidance. Philip argued that machines should be designed to fit the man, not vice versa. Long afterwards, I was myself promoting this idea at the Furniture Development Council.

Philip had been at Cambridge as an undergraduate between 1909 and 1914. He was an American but lived in England. He and his wife, Lella, also American, kept open house in Chesterton Road. He introduced me to the Heretics, founded in 1909 as a result of a paper by Dr W. Chawner, entitled, 'Prove all things'. The objects of the society were to promote 'discussion on problems of religion, philosophy and art'. Appeals to 'authority' were not permitted. Philip also introduced me to Henry Morris, and so changed my life.

Cambridge allowed time for nonsense too.

Gip Wells, who was at Oundle, introduced me to the Tea Pots. Once a year we purported to invite to a meeting a well-known personage to give a paper. The minutes of the previous meeting were read and, since there had been no such meeting, we had plenty of time to compile an account of a witty and intelligent discussion. The title of one non-existent paper was 'A plea for the weak, noisy man'.

One May weekend, to promote the return of leisurely study, we called a meeting of the 'Student pavement movement' for twelve o'clock on King's Parade. It was a great success. The sun shone and King's Parade was crowded with undergraduates sitting down on the road and pavements, reading, writing, playing cards, having a late breakfast. When the somewhat puzzled police asked us to move on, we did so with the greatest courtesy and then sat down again somewhere else – a most orderly affair.

Another time we hired the Guildhall for Sir Arthur Conan Doyle to speak on 'Materialisations', to be followed by a discussion on 'Spirits in Everyday Life', and 'Sex Equality after Death'. Tickets were sent to several dons. The announcement had gone out only a few days before the meeting; nevertheless the Guildhall was full and there were even some dons on the platform. After five or ten minutes my job was to pull the string that lowered a large notice. The dons and others on the platform could not see it but those in the body of the hall could. The notice read 'We very much regret that Sir Arthur Conan Doyle has failed to materialise.' He was, at the time, in Canada.

4. The non-materialization of Sir Arthur Conan Doyle: scene in the Guildhall, Cambridge, c. 1920

Meanwhile, I had two years in which to get my degree. I concentrated on engineering when I first arrived at Cambridge, but all the time I was getting more and more interested in economics. Marshall and Pigou were the set books. Many of my friends, notably Trevor Fenwick and George Dickinson, seemed to know chapter and paragraph and how to answer examination questions, but I found this approach difficult. I was getting more and more interested in John Maynard Keynes and his series of supplements to the *Manchester Guardian* on the reconstruction of Europe.

5. Molly and friend sunbathing at Cambridge

As the time approached for the examination I was getting somewhat alarmed at not knowing the set books sufficiently well. I need not have worried, however. The examiners had been changed, and the new ones were not so much concerned with orthodox answers to orthodox questions as with answers to real problems.

6. With my brother Fleetwood (left) and twin sisters Nancy and May at Craven Cottage, Southwold, about 1913

But there was a new complication. A naval friend was to be married at Caterham and wanted me to be present – the wedding was to be at 2.30 on the same day as my final paper, which would end at 12.00. I could hire a three-passenger aeroplane. The problem was how to pay for it. I had a friend who was interested in photography and thought that he could manage to get exclusive photographs of the wedding – it was to be something of a Society occasion – so he took a one-way ticket. My brother and another friend also took one-way tickets from London to Cambridge, and my mother, bless her, took a return. The final examination paper was on the economics of transport! As I wrote, I heard my aeroplane flying over. I simply could not help writing about my proposed journey and comparing it with other forms of transport.

When the results of the examination came through I was delighted at getting a Second in engineering and particularly at getting a First in economics. It was not, of course, an honours degree; but although the post-war slump was on the horizon I felt reasonably confident of getting a job.

While at Cambridge, I travelled to London by train, canoe, by air (as I have already mentioned) and by bicycle.

The canoe journey was during the Easter vacation. We used two Canadian-type canoes. With me in one of the canoes was Julian Fry and in the other were Ken Laurie and Tim Kanthack. We went up the Granta into the Cam to Newport with a portage across to the Stort and then down through Bishops Stortford into the Stort navigation and into the

Lee through Hoddesdon, then by Whitechapel Cut through the lock gates at Wapping Old Stairs into the Thames.

The journey to London took about four days and it was dusk when we arrived at Wapping Old Stairs. It was cold and drizzling and the tide was beginning to ebb. Julian had been taken ill and it was hard work paddling on my own. So I had to leave him at a pub on the river. A police boat helped me some of the way and I finished at Cadogan Pier, where I met the others who had arrived some time before me. I then caught the number 24 bus home to Hampstead.

We returned by the Grand Union Canal, up and over the Chilterns. Near Fenny Stratford, there was a short portage to the Ousel, not much more than a small brook. On the way, the river took us through a garden. On asking permission, I was greeted by 'Certainly, Mr Pritchard.' They had read in the papers that we were returning to Cambridge a different way and they had guessed our route. They were charming, gave us tea and dried our clothes (one of the canoes had capsized). Then the Bedford Ouse, through Bedford, St Neots and St Ives to Erith, then along the old west river, not much more than a stagnant stream, into the Cam at the Fish and Duck and on to Cambridge – a round trip of just nine days.

4
More Cambridge and early jobs

Cambridge University Appointments Board was helpful. Although unemployment was high and still increasing, I was full of optimism.

7. The canoe trip: a stop at Olney on the Ouse, en route from Cambridge to London. Second on the left is Julian, son of Roger Fry

Two influences were pulling at me. Philip Sargent Florence's lectures on industrial psychology suggested industry, and Henry Morris was urging me to go in for local government and education.

I was offered a job with the Lewis Group of department stores in Liverpool and Manchester. My brother, Fleetwood, was strongly in favour; I decided against.

The Michelin Tyre Company were looking for three or four graduates to be trained in their methods. During my interview we talked about economics, trade unions and industrial efficiency. I was offered a job at £300 a year. I would first get six months' training in Clermont-Ferrand and then, if I was any good, I might get an appointment anywhere in the world. I took the job but asked to be paid in sterling, in London; the franc was fluctuating but always downwards against the pound. They agreed, and this paid off rather well.

At the factory, the training department was run by a Monsieur Bougarde, a comfortable buffer with a sense of humour. He taught us time study, starting with the most simple movements. At first it seemed childish, but gradually we began to understand what they were teaching us – the ability to observe detail accurately, a scientific approach, not unlike the substance of Philip Florence's lectures.

We then learned how to break down a series of operations into units and record the time of each; we could then see where to improve or if possible eliminate a movement to save time. The emphasis was on the importance of a factual approach to any problem.

8. Myself as a young man, in an Inverness cape belonging to my father

The firm's general policy was to pay just above the average rates, provide good conditions and a generous pensions policy and then demand hard work. There was continual propaganda about the privilege of being a member of Michelin. The firm certainly had a very high reputation in France.

I was enjoying myself and gaining confidence, though still failing to get on with the language. Our hotel was pleasant but expensive, so I moved down into the town to a room in a grand but delapidated house in the Cours Sablon. My room had large french windows opening out on to an unkempt garden, with a fountain that just worked – and a reasonable supply of insects! I wrote to my mother asking how to get rid of them.

In December I was offered a job in England at £450 a year, and took it. On returning to England I was stationed at the Michelin office in Kensington. My first job was to find out why British motorists, who used the Michelin itineraries for travelling on holiday, did not use them again the next year. Was it because of dissatisfaction? It was an interesting and useful experience in market research that helped to decide policy.

Sometimes the firm made strange mistakes. They had men employed to note what makes of tyres were on what makes of cars. The results showed that in London almost 40 per cent of the cars were Rolls-Royces – someone had stationed the observers near Harrods.

I was given a somewhat similar job in Manchester, assessing motorists' opinions of different makes of tyres, how and why they chose, and what their reasons were. In the questionnaire I was given, one question near the top asked 'Do you like Michelin best?' I soon found this was a foolish question, so I put a reverse question at the bottom. 'Do you like Dunlop best?' A high proportion of the motorists asked answered 'Yes' to both questions.

While in Manchester, I remembered a Lancashire industrialist I had met; so one weekend I went to see him and stayed the night. He said that if I wanted a job I should go and see his managing director. The conversation with the managing director went well. I was asked if I was thinking of getting married; yes, I was. Had I anyone in mind? Yes, I had. After further talk I believed I had been offered a well-paid job with good prospects, so I went back to my hotel and wrote two letters, one accepting the offer and asking when I should join the firm, and the other to Michelin, resigning.

Michelin replied at once, saying they were sorry I was leaving, and would I prefer to work out my month's notice or to go straight away, adding that of course, I would have my pension. The other letter was not answered. I wrote again, but again there was no reply. I was now out of work.

When I complained to a friend of my experience, he laughed. He too had been offered a job there; but he was also told by the great man that he was looking for a son-in-law.

I was out of work for several months and that was no fun. I could, of course, live at home in Hampstead with my mother. I spent the time answering advertisements and being interviewed. Some of the firms I applied to and visited were interesting. I had my name down with a private employment agency and there was a job vacant at Venesta. Venesta was concerned with buying and correlating purchases from different plywood mills in the Baltic and elsewhere. I was turned down, but the chairman had made a note of my address.

Meanwhile I was offered a job on *The Field* magazine, selling advertising space, and took it. Later I remembered Frere Reeves, a 'Tea Pot' at Cambridge who was now editor of the magazine *World Today*. Frere gave me the job of advertisement manager, a high-sounding name for someone selling advertising space – but I had a free hand and was not tied to a list of firms as I had been at *The Field*.

Being at *World Today* provided sufficient money, which, together with what Molly had, was just enough to get married on. A few months later, in 1925, I was asked to go back to Venesta for another interview; that was the start of one of the most fruitful experiences of my life.

5
Henry Morris

As I have mentioned, it was through Philip Florence that I met Henry Morris, who had just been appointed secretary to the County Education Committee. I soon became a frequent, rather shy visitor to his rooms in Trinity Street. On his Sunday walks, there would be three or four of us taking our sandwiches and having beer in a pub. It was usually an occasion for a monologue by Henry developing his ideas.

9. Henry Morris, Chief Education Officer for Cambridgeshire and instigator of the Village Colleges, about 1938

It was almost impossible to interrupt him. On one occasion, when he was despising mediocrity, cheap substitutes and insincerity in design, he saw a particularly sentimental gnome in the garden of a pub; he swiped at it with his stick and off came its head. That stopped him for a moment.

Henry would frequently talk of the needs for a far wider-based education. He pointed to other social agencies that in his view ideally should be closely linked. His ideas were soon taking shape and by 1924 he produced a Memorandum under the title 'The Village College'. He listed the various related agencies that were already under the responsibility of the County Council and by lucid argument led the reader to see how and why they should all be linked together. He pointed out that the County Council was the statutory authority for education from elementary to further education including agriculture and social and physical training for all ages. It was also responsible for public libraries, juvenile employment and unemployment insurance, as well as public health, agriculture and other rural industries. By bringing together all these activities under one roof and administration, including facilities for women's institutes, the British Legion, choral classes and girl and boy scouts, the Village College was an imaginative invention. Alfred Fordham, who later became chairman of the County Education Committee, said of the Memorandum that 'it was one of the most remarkable pieces of work that had been done for a long time'. By February 1925 it was unanimously accepted. Henry had only been secretary of the Committee for two or three years.

The Memorandum is a fine piece of writing. Henry leads his reader on step by step to the Village College as a cultural centre, providing education for life. 'There would be no leaving school,' he writes; 'after prenatal advice the child would enter at three and leave only at extreme old age.' He adds that the school leaving age might well be raised to ninety!

'The Village College would provide an opportunity for creative architecture', he maintains, and Henry goes on to point out that 'there has been no public architecture in the English countryside since the Parish Churches were built in the middle ages' apart from asylums, workhouses and poor schools – 'a sight to put all heaven in a rage'.

Henry was invited to meet Lord Eustace Percy, then President of the Board of Education. Here was his opportunity to persuade the Minister to encourage the Village College idea for the whole country.

Henry stayed at our little flat in London. He put on what he called an 'administrative collar' with wings. Mrs Curzon, our daily, had to help him tie his tie. He returned that evening indignant and furious. I am told that, on welcoming Henry, 'Lord Useless Percy' said; 'Well now, Mr Morris, what is this pretty little bauble you have come to see me about?' It 'was just not good enough'.

Plans for the first college were being prepared for the village of Sawston, but when Henry showed them to us, Molly and I were disappointed. The plans were competent and pleasant but looked to the past for inspiration. This was hardly Henry's 'opportunity for creative architecture'. But the very fact that his ideas were being put into practice was a wonderful achievement. Sawston was opened by the Prince of Wales in October 1930 – just six years after Henry had presented his Council with his Memorandum.

All the time, Henry's taste in art was broadening. He appreciated, perhaps as an intellectual exercise, much of the best in the early modern architecture, but he was puzzled at what he saw illustrated of the work of Le Corbusier and of Walter Gropius and his colleagues at the Bauhaus. But when Gropius arrived in England in 1934, three more colleges had just been agreed. So I arranged for Gropius and Henry to meet at the Lawn Road Flats. In spite of Gropius's poor English they obviously understood each other.

Although he was anxious for Gropius to design the next village college,

10. Impington Village College by Gropius and Fry, Walter Gropius's only significant commission in England in the 1930s

at Impington, and although he was more than ever insistent on the importance of the visual and the physical surroundings as a powerful civilizing influence, Henry seemed almost at a loss to find the way through the opposition which was growing in the county. He believed that the only way to persuade his Committee was to find someone or some group to offer to pay Gropius's fee. His Committee had probably never heard of Walter Gropius anyway. Why pay extra fees when they had a staff architect?

We had just three or four weeks to find some £1,200 (a lot of money in those days). My secretary for Isokon Furniture, Joan Walton, did hardly anything else but type appeal letters drafted by Henry. Within two weeks we had about half the money, raised from many different sources; Henry then had no hesitation in joining with me to guarantee the remainder. But when it was known that Gropius and Fry had been appointed we found it more difficult to complete the fund, and it took several years.

When Henry saw the revised plans for Impington, he wrote to his friend Charles Fenn: 'Gropius's plans are superb, a veritable architectural

11. Entrance at Impington. The building was completed in 1939, after Gropius had left England

seduction.' (He was also good at abuse: he described Reginald Bloomfield's Regent Street as being 'carelessly excreted by some prehistoric monster in a moment of sadness'.)

Gropius's design for Impington, with its great corridor, created a building in which Henry Morris's theories could be realized. The corridor was the centre and passageway through which all, young and old, would meet and pass. Henry was fond of saying it was important to 'significate' ideas and occasions.

It was one of his great disappointments that Henry Moore's family group, now in Stevenage, did not find its way to Impington. The first ideas for this group were worked out for Impington to express the continuing importance of the family in the whole Village College idea. Morris loved happy families with children, and was sad that, being homosexual, he would never marry and have a family himself.

It is difficult to write about Henry Morris in a few words. There is so much to describe – the beauty of his spoken and written word, his love of music, his love of colour, his intolerance of mediocrity, his scorn alike for the sterility of the British Communists and for 'Capitalists with faces like plates', his high religious attitude to life and his scorn for the 'mumbo jumbo of orthodoxy', his love for the singing in King's College chapel, his love for the young family. 'My ambassadors for the future' he said of our grandchildren not long before he died at the age of seventy-three.

I had early on become a loving disciple. When the end came we had a small dinner party in our flat, with other 'disciples' – Ian Philips, Harry Rée, Tom Lupton, David Hardman – telling each other stories of Henry. From that meeting sprang the Henry Morris Memorial Trust to give travelling scholarships to students of the Village Colleges.

A total side of Henry's attitude was summed up in a letter to his friend Charles Fenn:

> Reading much, trying to get to know more science, eugenics, evolution and that trump card of our species, cause and effect. Also trying to appreciate more art... architecture, town planning, the ordering of the environment, poetry too, drama, music. The truth is there is no reality but science and art and the only pursuit in life is to bathe in them as one's constant medium. There is only one cure for civilisation – more and more of it.

The influence of Henry Morris has been strong.

During the war, Jacquetta Hawkes and Sammy Cooke, who was a tenant at the Lawn Road Flats, managed to get Henry invited to speak to the committee of the post-war reconstruction secretariat of the Cabinet Office. Jacquetta said the impact of his speeches was terrific.

12. Molly with Henry Morris in the early 1920s

In October 1954, Bassingbourne, the last Village College to be conceived, born and completed before Henry's retirement, was opened. R.A.Butler, who was then Chancellor of the Exchequer, came to perform the opening ceremony, much to the surpise of the locals.

Butler gave a fine tribute. 'I would in many ways', he said, 'rather have behind me the sort of educational record that Mr Morris has than the dreadful toil and trouble of the life I now lead.' He had been responsible for the Education Act of 1944, which brought about what Henry Morris described as 'almost a silent revolution'. When the Act was being drafted Morris had been sent for. 'I am quite certain that my experience on that occasion had a profound impression on my mind when I came to plan the Education Act of 1944, and therefore I feel I am coming back today to pay a small debt of gratitude,' said Butler.

David Hardman, Norman Fisher and I wrote to R.A.Butler asking for a high honour for Henry – he had a CBE, but we believed more should be done. But there was some strange, never-revealed blockage; perhaps it was that he was a homosexual. Henry had a nagging feeling that he had not really been accepted, and this led to his desire for an honour. In later years, when, in Hill End Hospital, he was getting confused, a friend heard him murmur: 'I was worth a CH.'

Henry applied his last remaining energies to Digswell Art Trust, where young artists and craftsmen were provided with a flat and studio at favourable terms. There is an account of Digswell in Harry Rée's book on Henry. But soon even that was getting beyond him. Again he had to go back to hospital.

He made good progress and with the help of Dr Stevenson, the most understanding head of Hill End, it was arranged that we could take Henry to the Evelyn Nursing Home in Cambridge. While he was there, I was asked if he was well enough to open the next Village College. I knew he was not, but I knew also how much he would like to be asked, so I advised yes, and immediately asked David Hardman if he would be ready to stand in. To everybody's alarm Henry began preparing his speech. He ordered the Council car to fetch him. He gave his speech, not once but three times. Once he turned his back on the audience and spoke to those on the platform, who included many distinguished people – the Bishop and, I believe, the Lord Lieutenant. Mrs Parsons, the Chairman of the Education Committee, stopped him charmingly, saying: 'Mr Morris, you have given a splendid speech, now sit down and have a rest.' This he quietly did. That was his last public speech.

Although Henry was really past travel, Graham Arnold courageously volunteered to take him to Italy, for Henry was longing for the sun and the beauty of the architecture. The love of beauty in all forms was fundamental to his life. Italy gave him more than great pleasure, it was almost a kind of orgasm. 'We must go to Florence – I must see more art, beauty, architecture – Giotto, Fra Angelico, Chianti, food – food, the edible art, light, colour and love.'

After such a visit he was recharged and wrote; 'I am, at last, well, and could seduce a lamp post.'

It was not long before Henry had to be moved back to Hill End. This was one of the saddest times of all, with only echoes of the real Henry.

David Hardman once found Henry apparently asleep; but suspecting that he wasn't, he kept on saying, 'Henry, it's me, David. I have come to see you. Don't you know who I am?' After that had been repeated a few times Henry murmured, 'Only too well.'

And when John Dugdale came, who much admired Henry and his work but had not given as much support to Henry's schemes as he thought he should, he also found Henry apparently asleep. When he eventually made him understand, Henry murmured, 'About time too.'

The voices were almost from the grave.

The last time I saw him alive I was overwhelmed with sadness – we were saying goodbye. He had a look of half understanding.

One of the inmates called out in his desolation, 'I wish I could go home.' The cry was taken up by all the others, and amongst them was the voice of Henry Morris – 'So do I, so do I.'

He should have gone sooner. He will not be forgotten.

THE THIRTIES

6
Venesta

One of the most significant things that happened during my ten years at Venesta was hearing of the Bauhaus and Walter Gropius. It influenced much of my future.

Venesta was associated with a firm called Luterma, which had factories in Finland, Lithuania, Estonia and, before the war, in Moscow. The managing director of Luterma was Martin Luther – said to be a direct descendant of *the* Martin Luther. I came to have a great respect for him, and besides, he had a sense of humour. He was rescued, with others, from the Luterma factories by a British gunboat during an uprising in Estonia in the 1914–18 war.

Apparently the original arrangement between Venesta and Luterma had arisen from the need to find a suitable method of packing tea; plywood was found to be an appropriate material. When I first joined Venesta, in September 1925, I was asked to see what could be done to increase the sales of plywood hatboxes and suitcases. These were made in Estonia, of bright yellow polished plywood; the edges were joined and held secure by long, thin metal angle pieces, efficient and strong. Neither hatbox nor suitcase sold well in England. Someone had suggested giving them a dark finish that might be described as oak colour. They sold no better. Then someone suggested trying a burnt finish. This was done in the hot press; the result was pleasing and needed little or no polish since it was not easy to stain, but these sold no better. Then a pattern was put on to the hot plate – someone said it was not unlike leather but still the sales of suitcases did not increase. The catalogue described it as embossed to represent imitation crocodile leather. Being in charge of advertising, I left in that true description.

Wells Coates had arrived in England from Canada in 1929, and I first met him when he called at the Venesta office in Vintry House. Plywood was then regarded as a cheap substitute for solid wood, even by some of those in the firm, and while I was principally employed to advertise and promote existing Venesta products, I believed it was important to find uses where its intrinsic qualities could be used. Wells Coates was using plywood for just those reasons for the Cresta factory in Welwyn Garden City. Here was an opportunity for back-scratching. Venesta could show photographs of the use of plywood in a modern setting and Wells would get the publicity.

When we needed an advertising agent the selection was a problem. In

13. Wells Coates in 1937

those days the agents could be roughly divided into two groups. The first consisted of those whose main interest was the selling of space in journals with little consideration as to how to fill the space. The other group professed to advise their customers on which journals were the most suitable and how to get their story across in the most effective manner. Some agents were even beginning to use market research. My brother was amongst the latter group, concerned with a serious approach to advertising, and with a few others he had formed a society called the Waggoners: they hitched their wagon, so they said, to the stars. Fleetwood and I were referred to as the highbrow brothers since I was also getting bald.

Fleetwood and his partners, Sinclair Wood and John Gloag, were taking the problem of selling and marketing as a total problem. It was not easy to select, but I believed Fleetwood, particularly with Gloag, had an edge over the others.

The chairman and managing director of Venesta was Henry Rutherford, tall, handsome and economical of speech. Working in the same office was Graham Reid, a younger man who had been in the Army.

I discussed the problem of advertising with Rutherford. He listened and then said that, since I was in charge of advertising, it was my business to make the choice and he could later judge if my choice was right – a good example of delegation. My previous training at Michelin had been salutary and useful, especially for a young man just down from university. There I had learnt the importance of measuring business activity objectively. Now I had the chance to apply what I had learnt.

The grading of plywood was based on the number of knots and discolorations on each side of a board, each mill describing them as A/B or B/B, etc. Their grading might vary from time to time. Venesta decided to define, standardize and name each grade. The names used were, for example, Nilnot, Specnot, Noknot. Thus the buyer would know precisely what he was buying.

The standard grading system was introduced in the late 1920s or early 1930s and was useful for large-scale buyers and timber merchants and their customers alike. Some at Venesta wondered if the extra costs involved in the grading and labelling, plus the advertising, were justified. During the period of falling prices in the 1930s slump, we compared prices and qualities for plywood from our competitors and found that Venesta plywood, with its graded labels, held up better than our competitors' product. We were selling both reliable graded plywood and also 'reputation'. So again measured knowledge proved useful.

One of the most interesting technical developments was made by Dr Love, a scientist at Venesta. This was a method of fixing thin metal sheets to plywood, using galvanized steel, copper and Monel metal. The new material was called Plymax. Plymax had a fine flat surface suitable for painting and was remarkably rigid. Two-sided Plymax was some sixty times as rigid as sheet steel of the same weight (the plywood acted as the distance piece between the metal sheets, similar to a girder). Although it was found practical to manufacture the material, we had no clear idea of how and where it could be used; so, at John Gloag's suggestion, we placed an advertisement in *The Times*, describing the qualities of the new material and asking for suggestions for its use.

The suggestion that seemed the most promising was to use Plymax for the panels of light vans. In those days thin sheets of aluminium were often used for this purpose, but unless they were amply stiffened, the sheets became wavy and were no good for signwriting, and could also develop considerable drumming. Plymax, with its advantage of inherent rigidity and a fine flat surface, presented none of these problems.

Sales of Plymax for this purpose were an immediate success and rapidly increased, but it was not long before the sales curve began to flatten out. Some suggested more salesmen, others suggested increased advertising. Fortunately I was able to consult Robert Spicer, whom I knew through PEP; he was at the Society of Motor Manufacturers and Traders, in charge of statistics. It was possible from Robert's statistics to make a reasonable estimate of the cycle of van life and replacement and, therefore, an estimate of the size of our market. It soon became clear that we had achieved a high proportion of the total sales possible and that further promotional and sales effort would only result in diminishing returns for the increased expenditure. It was then decided to reduce sales expenditure on that market and search for new markets. The statistical approach had paid off.

In 1936 John Gloag produced a book on Plymax, showing a large variety of uses with full technical information. To demonstrate that very thin Plymax, not more than a quarter of an inch thick, unsupported except by hinges, could remain flat without warping, I designed a small sideboard. It had a Monel metal Plymax top and copper Plymax sides and doors. It is now in the Victoria and Albert Museum. I should have designed something with a larger door, perhaps a wardrobe.

We had noticed that in Europe the fully flush door was becoming popular, and we believed that it might catch on in Britain too. Since flush doors provided another new use for plywood, I decided to visit Germany with Wells Coates and Serge Chermayeff in 1931 to find out more.

Serge had arranged that we would meet Eric Mendelsohn in Berlin. Mendelsohn took us round the building he had designed for the Metal Workers' Union (their president was Herr Ebert, soon to be president

14. Sideboard designed by myself c. 1930 to demonstrate the rigidity of Plymax metal-faced plywood. Because of its uncompromising appearance this design has always been referred to as 'The Oven'

of the first German Republic). All the doors down the corridors were flush and made of built-up timber.

The next day we went to see Gropius's Bauhaus in Dessau. Since I had been experimenting with new approaches in the use of plywood, the Bauhaus was of particular interest to me. The development there in thinking anew about established materials had been impressive, and I had believed that a visit to the Bauhaus would be useful. But by this time the Bauhaus was in the throes of the political difficulties which led to the closure of the Dessau building in October 1932, and the school, when we got there, was more or less deserted. Gropius himself had resigned three years earlier. All the same, the Bauhaus looked fine amid the unkempt grass, and at least we could look round the building, which, in itself, had a very powerful impact on me. I did not know it then, but both the Bauhaus and Walter Gropius were to have an enormous influence on much of my future.

We saw much else in Germany, and there was no doubt of the rapid development and use of built-up timber boards; laminate and block boards were the most common, used in both building and furniture. We returned to London, and I made my report to Venesta about what we had seen and what seemed to me to be the future trend in housing requirements in connexion with plywood products. A low-priced flush door was clearly one of the products to be considered and already Dr Love was thinking about ways to produce such a door.

The conventional joinery method would either be a solid door, perhaps using block board, or a hollow door consisting of plywood on a timber frame. The timber would be joined by mortice and tenon. Dr Love was not convinced that the mortice method was the best way and tried placing the timber members on a sheet of plywood, just butt joined; another sheet of plywood was then placed on top and the whole assembly put into the press. The performance was clumsy and difficult but the result was satisfactory. It was next decided to hold the frame members together with corrugated nails, their only function being to keep the frame members safely joined while the complete assembly was put into the press.

Trials were made comparing this and the conventional method of mortice and tenon. Both methods were satisfactory, and the proportion of doors that warped was small: but strangely, there was a slightly higher proportion of failure from the conventional door, suggesting that the mortice and tenon might indeed not be the best method, besides being the more costly. It was decided to go ahead with the production of the Venesta Flush Door. Max Fry, the architect – and later Gropius's partner – designed an easy way to fix legs to the hollow door so that it had an alternative use – as a table.

Finding ways to stimulate the new uses for plywood was rather fun. To show that conventional dovetail joining was unnecessary for plywood, I had a small box made that was joined with machine square dovetails. The dimensions of the box were such that two, placed one above the other, would equal three placed horizontally. The vertical boxes could take large books, and the horizontal boxes could take small ones. At that time book units had not developed far, so these boxes caused some interest; although they were meant simply to demonstrate possibilities in the use of plywood, we actually sold quite a few.

The factory in Estonia made seats for tram cars. These were made of plywood five or six feet long which could be made in many different profiles. In 1933 I designed a chair and had it made to demonstrate the firmness and flexibility of the curve.

Soon after that, I was sent out to tackle the timber and builders' merchants. I was nervous of going out on the road to sell. What if I was not successful? On the other hand, the new grading policy was somewhat my own baby and I believed in it.

I was also to try to establish agents for the new Venesta Flush Door. I did not do as badly as I had feared. One of my first and best successes was with Atkinson of Leeds, builders' merchants. Edgar Atkinson, the managing director, was a typical Yorkshire gentleman, very careful and slow to open up and slow to commit himself. I fixed a sole agency for the Venesta Flush Door for a specified area and we did quite well together.

I was then sent to Paris for three to four months to make a report on the French branch of Luterma. They had a factory at Le Bourget where they made gaboon (okourme) plywood. The French assignment was difficult (as my French was very poor), but a valuable experience; superficially conditions were similar to those in Britain, but I soon found that trading in France was very different and that to introduce into France the marketing methods we had used at home would not do. Fortunately I had an old friend from London who was working in the Paris branch of Crawford Advertising, and I could learn from their experiences. Through him I came across Louise Goepfert again – I had got to know Louise through Beatrix Tudor Hart in London. Louise was working in Fontainebleau at a strange institute run by Gurdjieff. We got on well together and she asked me to go down for a weekend. It was a fascinating experience.

Gurdjieff had established an Institute for the Harmonic Development of Man in the villa at Fontainebleau given to Dreyfus as part compensation for what he had not done. A number of Gurdjieff's disciples had gathered there; Dorothy Massingham was one of them. If a disciple was an intellectual Gurdjieff would give him manual work to do and vice versa. Dorothy had some form of tuberculosis and so she was given her lodgings on a platform over the horses in the stable.

15. Venesta stand at the Building Trades Exhibition designed by Le Corbusier, Pierre Jeanneret and Charlotte Perriand in 1930

16. Later stands for Venesta by Lubetkin, 1934 (top), and Wells Coates, 1931 (below)

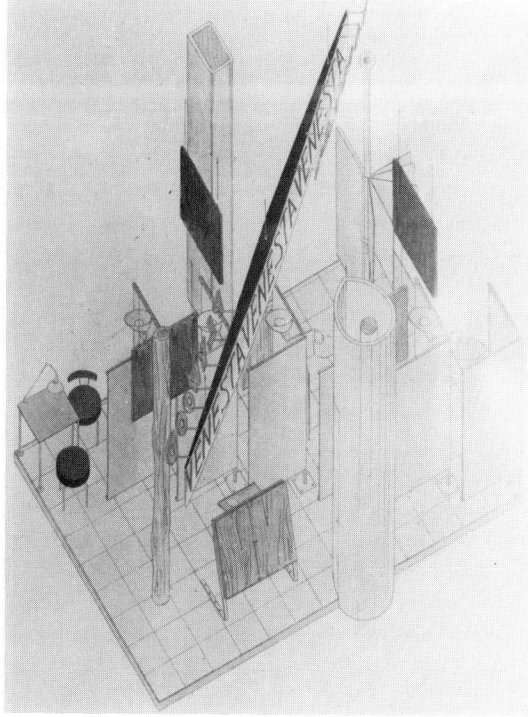

When I asked to see the great man, I was told that he was in the office – the Grand Café in the main street of Fontainebleau. I found him there, with a Dutch friend of mine, in earnest conversation and drinking what Gurdjieff called 'the divine liquid Armagnac'. After drinking nine glasses of this divine liquid the great man said that the women would have finished and it was time to go.

Off we went to the Turkish bath. It had been dug out of a hill in the grounds of the villa by the disciples. Gurdjieff asked me if I had the English complaint. I did not know what that was but I was instructed to sit next to him at the end of the bench. I soon found that I was in a very hot corner and it was impossible to move past the very large Gurdjieff. We then had to have a cold shower, which was also some kind of test, and Gurdjieff seemed a little disappointed that I obviously enjoyed it. After the shower we went into a large space with a dome painted by various disciples. Benches were placed all round, and in the centre was a large, slightly sloping slab of marble. Gurdjieff was placed on his stomach on the slab and then his brother, a veritable picture of a eunuch, even larger and fatter than Gurdjieff, with red-rimmed eyes and bald, led in a small boy who walked up each of Gurdjieff's legs, over his buttocks and down again, waggling his toes as he went. Then a larger boy was brought in to do the same, and then a larger one. Finally his brother came and walked up over his body and shoulders.

At the supper that followed, Gurdjieff told me that he liked the English zeros. I came to understand that he meant a cheque made out in his name with as many noughts as possible after the first figure. He told me that I should have a slice of cold potato with a special powder; I realized he was teasing me again – it was curry powder. I did not want to be defeated, so I took it in one go and drank as much water and wine as I could. Luckily I was not troubled. After supper we heard Gurdjieff read passages from his book *Beelzebub's Tales to his Grandson*. I saw Louise hardly at all.

While in Paris I was thinking about the forthcoming Building Trades Exhibition in London. On a previous visit to Paris I had been to the Petit Palais and had seen there an exhibit by Le Corbusier, Jeanneret and Perriand. It showed a full open plan for an apartment for two, bourgeois privacy arranged by cunning planning. I was so struck by it that I wondered about asking them to design the Venesta stand for the exhibition. It seemed a cheek to ask such a famous firm to design a small exhibition stand, but with the encouragement of John Gloag I plucked up courage and went to see Pierre Jeanneret, a cousin of Le Corbusier. To my delight they agreed and Charlotte Perriand was to do the job. Although the stand was small, it was a striking exhibit which made a clear demonstration of our grading policy. Later Venesta had two other exhibition stands designed by famous architects: Wells Coates, and Lubetkin of Tecton.

17. Alvar Aalto, whose buildings in Finland in the 1930s impressed me greatly

18. Myself (back view, right) with P. Morton Shand and Aalto at the Paimio sanatorium, Aalto's most influential building, designed 1929–33

Around this time I applied for membership of the Architectural Association but was turned down because I was a tradesman.

One of my last jobs at Venesta was to visit, with Graham Reid and Morton Shand, the Luterma factories in the Baltic. Seeing the three factories was fascinating. The oldest, at Reval, made not only birch plywood but also furniture. Later they made parts of Breuer furniture for Isokon, among them the nesting tables and the stool. The Riga factory was the newest and most modern, with up-to-date costing and planning systems. In Riga I had the experience of drinking vodka the so-called Russian way. Full glasses were put in a row and you were supposed to see how far along the row you could go, emptying each glass as you went.

We flew to Helsinki and on to Lojo, to the other Luterma factory. Finland seemed all sand and lakes, but the manager Lementie's garden had a rich black soil and he was growing currants and other fruits and vegetables. We found that in spite of his claims that the soil was natural, he had been scraping out the vats of blood albumen, which was then used for cementing the plywood, and spreading it on his garden like a fertilizer. From Helsinki we went on to see the sanatorium designed by Alvar Aalto – one of the most influential buildings of its day – and then on to Obo to see the furniture factory where his furniture was being made.

I had already told Rutherford that I was going to resign from Venesta in order to spend more time on the development of Isokon. In many ways I was sorry to go. Rutherford gave me a retainer for a few years – a charming and generous act and a great help to me now that I was on my own.

7
PEP

The publication of Gerald Barry's *Week End Review* of 14 February 1931 led to the formation of PEP (Political and Economic Planning).

Gerald Barry had been editor of the *Saturday Review*, but when it changed hands he was ordered to toe the line of Beaverbrook's Empire Free Trade policy. He refused, resigned in March 1930 and set up the *Week End Review*. A year later, as a supplement to his new journal, he published *A National Plan for Great Britain*, a kite-flying exercise compiled by a young man on his staff, Max Nicholson, who was to be a key figure in the early phase of PEP.

During the years between the end of the war and the publishing of the *National Plan*, the nation as a whole seemed to be losing its way. There had been a short boom and great expectations, hopes for better working conditions, and more and better education, research, housing and welfare. Then the boom was played out and unemployment began to rise.

Discontent was growing and coming to a head. The Government was in a strong position to face trouble. It came on 3 May 1926 when the General Strike was called.

I had been at my job at Venesta for a only a few months. Work stopped at the warehouse in Millwall and in the factory at Silvertown, and there was little or nothing to do in the office.

I took time off and spent a week-end at Cambridge. Visiting Philip and Lella Florence, I again met Maurice Dobb, an economist friend, who almost believed that the strike would lead to the great revolution.

The strike in fact was in the main orderly, the telephone service operated as usual and so did food deliveries. There were a few outbreaks, promoted by the forerunners of the Fascists, trying to provoke trouble amongst angry workers.

I was now firmly left of centre. During the strike the Government produced a well-printed daily under the title *British Gazette*, using the presses of the *Morning Post*. The TUC produced the *British Worker* from the *Daily Herald* press. I helped in the distribution of the latter to areas outside London.

At first collecting the *British Worker* was easy, but very soon the paper boys realized that there was a shortage of papers to sell on the streets of London. When we were loading bundles into our open four-seater Lea Francis they managed, almost as a game and in good humour, to intercept the bundles that had to be thrown from the dispatch department across the pavement to the car. We countered by borrowing a van, and by backing it up over the pavement against the wide open dispatch doors.

The van was then driven to the suburbs where we met other distributors.

With Jack Neap, later a QC, we drove supplies of the *British Worker* to Leicester. I had obtained a TUC pass for the windscreen from Ben Tillett at the TUC office in Eccleston Square. I did not always use the label; it rather depended on the character of the area where I was driving.

Our instructions were to drive to the railway station, ask the picket where to find the Council of Action and deliver the papers only to them. At the Council of Action we delivered the papers. Jack Neap gave a stirring left wing address but the chairman, a trade unionist, interrupted with 'Stop that revolutionary nonsense. The city is under control and that is enough for the present.'

The end of the strike came suddenly on 12 May. Many on the right gloated, but some were anxious and began to think anew and try to find ways to repair the broken goodwill in industry and in the nation.

By the summer of 1931 the number of those unemployed was still rising: it was now three million. Foreign loans had to be found to help support the pound. The May Committee, formed in 1931, called for drastic economies and further cuts in salaries and wages.

Keynes, in the *New Statesman and Nation* of 15 August, wrote: 'The Committee showed no evidence of having given a moment's thought to the possible repercussions of their programme either on the volume of employment or on the receipts of taxation.' Later at a House of Commons Committee he referred to the report as 'the most foolish document I have ever had the misfortune to read'.

The Government fell on 21 August. There was dissatisfaction in all the parties and it was against this background that many of us began to think more deeply about politics, forming quite new ideas.

So it can be seen how the publication of Nicholson's *National Plan* provided a focal point and led to the formation of PEP. It was good journalism and came just at the right time. I became involved through Michael Young from Dartington. I went to the first meeting and met Max Nicholson for the first time. His enthusiasm was infectious.

There were two meetings I remember well. One was a dinner party at the Ivy on 15 March 1931 which was presided over by Sir Basil Blackett, a director of the Bank of England, with Sir Henry Bunbury, Julian Huxley, Max Nicholson, Gerald Barry, G.G. Whiskard and a few others.

Basil Blackett was proposing a new society to carry on the work sparked off by Barry and Max – he wanted a name that would suggest new ideas. 'The aim of the society,' he said 'would be concerned with political and economic planning.' I suggested, more as a joke than seriously, that the name might be just that, Political and Economic Planning, PEP for short. Blackett thought that was marvellous and the name was adopted.

In his memoirs Israel Sieff quotes an advertisement drafted by Clough Williams Ellis: 'PEP – try it in your bath.'

The other meeting I remember very well was at Dartington in April. Besides Max there was Sir Basil Blackett, Kenneth Lindsay and, I think, Whiskard and maybe one or two others. They all seemed very important and were somewhat aloof, and I felt isolated. We travelled down to Devon on the Saturday morning train.

Leonard Elmhirst met us at Totnes and showed us round the estate. We had tea and started work at 5.30 p.m.

In its agenda and terms of reference the meeting was long-winded, and although the proposed society was sparked off by Max's *National Plan*, the word 'plan' was only used once and the central aim of the society was defined as 'a co-ordinated conception of the problems involved in producing a National Plan, while its distinctive features in reorganization were on a basis of differentiated functions'.

That sounded fine – but what did it mean?

I had the impression that the new society would be more concerned with reforming existing institutions, government and industry rather than trying to understand the significance of planning and its implications – both important but separate problems.

The society's finances were a mystery. We were told that an enthusiastic but anonymous supporter would provide sufficient money to pay for a secretary and an office as a starter.

I had not then heard of the early plan to bring in Kenneth Lindsay with Elmhirst's finance, so I was disturbed by the secrecy surrounding his appointment as secretary. For a responsible body anonymous finance was unfortunate, especially since it was tied to a particular secretary.

After the Dartington weekend, work began, and the first Annual General Meeting of PEP was held at the Royal Society of Arts on 29 June 1931. Sir Basil Blackett reported that PEP was the outcome of the *Week End Review*'s *National Plan* and that a directorate had been formed consisting of Gerald Barry, Alfred Bossom, Henry Bunbury, Leonard Elmhirst, Julian Huxley, Laurence Neal, Israel Sieff, Josiah Stamp, G.G. Whiskard, with Kenneth Lindsay as a paid secretary and E.M.Nicholson (Max) as assistant secretary. Sir Basil was chairman.

Resolutions were passed in favour of planning. Planning must be compatible with personal and political freedom, and an attempt would be made by various groups in the society to draw up a comprehensive national plan by 3 June 1934.

Five groups were set up: Technique of Planning (later called Techplan), Public Utilities, Technique of Industrial Investment and Development, Social Services, Agricultural Research. Other groups were to be formed later.

Techplan, full of enthusiasm and the supreme confidence of youth (the average age of the members would have been about thirty), set out to tackle a world problem and to do so as a matter of great urgency. We were very serious.

The group consisted of A.E.Blake, a journalist with Communist tendencies; N.J.Gordon Clark, a director of a wine and spirits importers who was on the moderate right; Max Nicholson, who was the drafter; myself as chairman; N.W.Smith from one of the big banks; and Robert Spicer, the statistical economist from the Rubber Growers' Association. Ann Clayton (who was my secretary at Venesta) worked hard as an enthusiastic voluntary secretary. At times we called on Julian Huxley, Henry Morris and others.

Between the AGM on 29 June 1931 and the end of the year, Techplan had five weekend meetings (held from Friday to Sunday evenings, usually in the upstairs of a pub) and seven intensive evening meetings – we drove ourselves hard.

The weekends were exhausting but stimulating. First finding where we could all agree, then building up from that. This meant hard work for Max, drafting and redrafting each paragraph.

The opening paragraph of our first report was delightfully pompous: 'In view of the national emergency the following first interim report, containing provisional and tentative dates has been drawn up in advance of schedule. . . . A National Plan should be a part of a world plan.' We pointed out that any plan must have an aim or objective, it must be dynamic and adaptable. It must aim at maximum efficiency and the need to provide the maximum freedom for the individual.

We stressed the importance of flexibility and the importance of individual enterprise within an overall plan; performance should be checked against a time and progress schedule.

We believed that one of the first and essential jobs was to list and clarify the whole field of national activities. We drew up a table showing every activity we could think of, detailing the function of each. For this we made a splendid chart and called it the Python (although some called it the White Elephant). It went round three sides of a good-sized room.

The field for planning was treated on a two-dimensional basis: first, a horizontal classification covering the field from an occupational standpoint, and second, a vertical list dealing with functional activities.

In view of the subsequent events it is surprising that the directorate were taking so much notice of Techplan. The final report was formally presented to the chairman of PEP at a dinner meeting on 28 January 1932 at University College in Gower Street.

Meanwhile the self-appointed directorate seemed to be more and more concerned with finding ways to improve the *status quo* rather than thinking anew. We felt that our Techplan proposals were not being considered on their merits and that no attempt was made to understand them. At times some of us were for getting out and going on our own, but Max wanted to keep the group within the main structure of PEP, believing we might have a useful influence on the main body.

Some of the directorate believed that Techplan was trying to run away with PEP by proposing its plan for the organization for the society's groups. Apparently they did not know that the chairman had asked us to make proposals for ways to mobilize and allocate all PEP personnel. Communication was lax, perhaps deliberately so.

It was also about this time that there was the undercover move to get rid of Blackett and replace him with Sieff. Max wrote on 26 July 1932 that 'the conspirators in their impatience to be rid of Blackett have been quite ready to upset the whole programme of work and organization so as to place the official lead for the coming period in the hands of "Industry", i.e. Sieff and the reformers'.

The difference in attitude between the reformers and Techplan was now clear. The reformers were concerned to make the present industrial and social organizations more efficient. We in Techplan understood that PEP was concerned with planning, and that needed an objective. Was not that the original aim?

The reformers were wrongly assuming that we had in mind a fixed and rigid type of plan, whereas in our statements we were saying quite clearly that flexibility was of prime importance and that we believed free enterprise in many fields of activity would provide that flexibility.

In the spring of 1933 we had finished our work on Techplan. The final touching up of our document was done by Max and me on a ship touring up the Seine and back. That done, Max returned to PEP. Our work was published not by PEP, but by the New Atlantis under the title *A View on Planning*. PEP went on to produce many useful reports but not much concerned with the implication of national planning.

A View on Planning is divided into six main parts: the arguments, political limits, statement of assumption, economic basis, statement of principles, and concrete objective structure.

One of our statements has often helped to clear my mind. It took a long time before we could all agree on it, but once formulated it seemed so simple:

> Man must be regarded from three aspects. First, he is a person, unique, limited and short-lived. Second, he is a species, with an infinite expectation of life, and the capacity for evolutionary change. Third, he is a social organism possessing such a continuing tradition that neither the individual nor the species can function adequately except through the medium of the group.

Fifty years of PEP were celebrated by the publication of John Pinder's *Fifty Years of Political and Economic Planning*, and there was a meeting at the Royal Society of Arts on 29 June 1981, fifty years, almost to the hour, after the first Annual General Meeting, also held at the RSA. PEP has now been merged with the Policy Studies Institute. The Meeting's first speaker was Ralf Dahrendorf. *The Times* had asked Dahrendorf to review John Pinder's book but had sent the review back saying that, for reasons of policy, they were unable to publish it. Dahrendorf then proceeded to read the rejected review:

> With all its strengths, the British political tradition has two great weaknesses. One is the enjoyment of the adversary style in politics. . . . The other weakness is the prevailing time scale, which is surely shorter than that of any other Western democracy. Both together, the adversary style, the obsession with next week, perhaps the next budget, are reasons not only for serious mistakes, but also the absence of that confidence which is essential for a functioning policy and economy.

He then referred to PEP and the work that Max and I had done in what he called PEP's second version (Techplan):

> The second version of this plan, the Techplan, was so extraordinary that PEP denied parenthood and it was published independently under the unobtrusive title *A View on Planning* in December 1933. 'Planned economy, in one form or another, has plainly become inevitable for Western civilization,' its authors boldly affirm in the very first sentence. They then proceed to state in the most laconic form their assumptions and the implications for every aspect of economy and society. . . . The real triumph of PEP is that while there are many good reasons why it should have been discontinued decades ago – indeed while a fiftieth anniversary is not necessarily a reason for celebration for a policy research institute – it has in fact found

a new lease of life. The merger of PEP and CSSP has led to more than a combination of the two; it has led to the creation of an attractive centre of research and debate about issues of today and tomorrow. This is a remarkable achievement for which all those involved must be congratulated. It even justifies the otherwise somewhat perplexing subtitle of the anniversary volume: *Looking Forward 1931–1981*.

It was a good occasion, meeting old friends, good conversation. It reminded me of Henry Morris, who pointed out that professional, administrative and 'practical' men could not be trusted to run a country; it needed thinkers and those with imagination.

8
Children and education; Theta

Molly and I were married in August 1924; and since we were both in the early part of our careers, and fairly short of money, we did not plan on a family straight away. However, Molly became pregnant at just the wrong moment – just when she had been offered a job which she thought would suit her particularly well. However, she didn't even think of an abortion, and I was thrilled. This was early in 1926 and in the summer Molly told me I should keep the morning of Saturday 9 October free. Jonathan duly arrived at 6 a.m. on that day.

Bringing up our children was a great and serious adventure. Molly's mother, Rose, had worked at the infant welfare clinic in Marylebone. This was run by Dr Eric Pritchard (no relation), who advised a strict routine for feeding and potting. The child must be fed by the clock, pot-trained from the start, and never picked up except for nappy changing or feeding. The whole regime reminds me of a story about Molly's mother. On a hospital visit she met a poor woman who was to have an operation which would, in her words, 'take away the only pleasure we poor people have'.

Jonathan was a lusty, well-developed infant and, once he got used to the rather strict routine, he developed well, and was soon learning to walk with the aid of a walking frame which I invented.

However, it was a different story with Jeremy, who was born on 23 August 1928. He was smaller than Jonathan, and did not adapt to the strict routine. He had a poor appetite and was undersized through most of his childhood. On the other hand, his mental development, especially with reading and languages, was remarkably quick, while Jonathan seemed to have inherited some of my own problems with words. The relationship between a strong, sturdy elder brother who remained, for quite a long time, jealous of the newcomer, and an undersized younger one who could sometimes outwit him, was sometimes stormy.

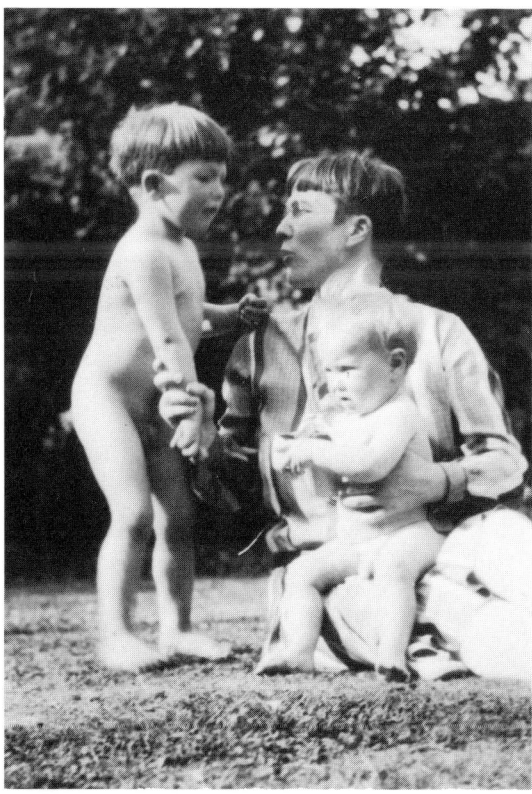

19. Molly with Jonathan and Jeremy in 1929

As the children grew up, we did a great deal of hard thinking about children, their upbringing and education. Molly became more and more interested in psychology, and eventually left her biochemical job to take up psychotherapy. Her close friend Doris Howard, whose son Ivor was born on the same day as Jonathan, had already done so. It was not long before Molly came to the conclusion that the regime of the boys' earlier days had been a bad mistake, and that a more lenient and affectionate treatment would have been better.

We were, in any case, inclined to question conventional ideas about education. Bertrand Russell's book *On Education* was published a few months before Jonathan was born, and we were both greatly influenced by it. At much the same time Portia Holman, whom we had met in Cambridge, introduced us to Beatrix Tudor Hart. She was a fine tall girl, handsome and intelligent and was passionately concerned with education. She would soon be working with the Russells and desperately wanted a child of her own. I was much impressed with her, and it was not long before I became the father of her daughter, Jennifer.

When Jonathan was about three we set up a nursery school on the top floor of our house in Platts Lane, to be run by Beatrix. This was very convenient for us and the boys, and gave them a splendid start. It was

20. Beatrix Tudor Hart and Jennifer

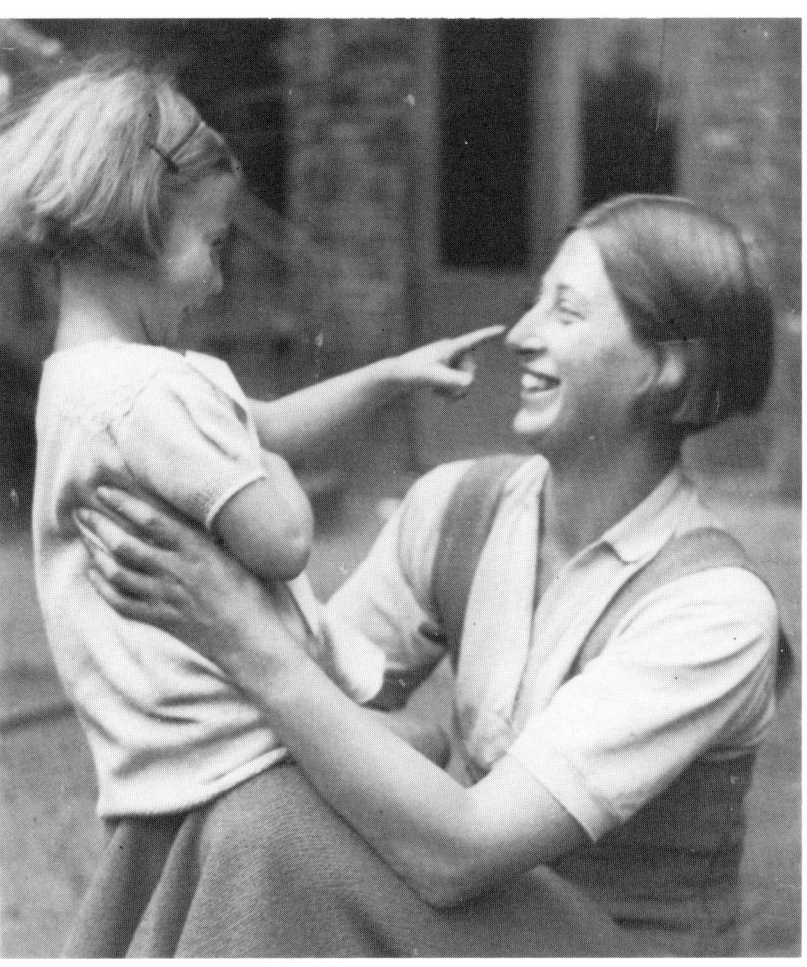

21. Myself with Jeremy

also a start for Beatrix, who ran her own school for the rest of her working life and has written illuminatingly about her ideas.

But what was to come after nursery school? With Molly and me both in full-time work, this seemed a puzzle. When the Russells founded their school on the Downs near South Harting, it seemed to be the ideal answer. We were not only enthusiastic about the Russells' ideas, but had already had a foretaste of Dora's maternal skills. When Jeremy was only three, the drains in our flat in Belsize Park went bad. We had to make a quick decision, so we asked Dora if she could have him for a few weeks. It seemed to work surprisingly well; Dora was a veritable mother-figure, and the family atmosphere she created was very real.

Beacon Hill school was exciting in many ways. The Russells had been influenced by Margaret Macmillan and her school for children of four to seven at Deptford, where the idea was to encourage the children to develop for themselves any need for discipline, rather than having discipline imposed on them. As a result, attendance at classes at Beacon Hill was voluntary, and the only compulsory rules were concerned with health – brushing your teeth and going to bed on time. The result was that the children went to class but sometimes objected to cleaning their teeth or going to bed.

Russell was a splendid teacher, and under his care the children became fascinated with numbers. One boy was a little slower than the rest and began lagging behind, and Russell suggested that the class slow down to allow him to catch up. The others would have none of it. So Russell suggested that the boy should have a book to help him. The boy said he couldn't read. A week or so afterwards he was found up a tree with a book, reading and catching up fast. No external discipline needed.

The school had a council, where the children really did make decisions; the Russells believed in letting them make mistakes if necessary and letting them learn the consequences. Later, when Jeremy was at a more conventional school in Hampstead, he was complaining about some rule, and we asked why he didn't take it up with the school council. He said that would be no good, since whatever the children decided, the master would have the last word. The council was useless.

I remain convinced that a measure of true self-government at school – especially at an early age – is a much more effective way of developing civilized habits than handing down orders. The children under self-government learn the rudiments of making decisions that affect others.

This was beautifully illustrated when we later visited Summerhill and met A.S. Neill. Apparently every few years the students had a kind of

22. With Molly, Jonathan and Jeremy examining an educational puzzle

23. Walking with Molly and the boys

revolution, and we arrived at just the right moment. There was to be a school meeting and it was being proposed that, as it was a free school, they should abolish all rules. We asked if we could attend; Neill put it to the children, and we were given permission to do so. The meeting was a serious and responsible discussion, and as it became clear that the vote would go in favour of abolishing all the rules, Neill asked if this would include the staff. Oh, yes, everyone in the school would be free. What about the laws of the state? The vote would apply only within the school grounds. It was duly carried.

Even before the vote, the smaller children were edging towards the door, and as soon as it was taken many rushed and put their belongings away. There was some mad pandemonium, and there was not much sleep that night.

Next morning there was no breakfast. Where was the cook? In bed – she had been disturbed in the night and had decided to sleep in. Eventually some food was put on the table; some got it, but many didn't. A queue was formed – the beginning of rules. Gradually, in the days that followed, the rules came back; the experience of finding out for themselves the importance of rules was surely valuable.

The children of Beacon Hill not only took decisions for themselves but

24. Beatrix picnicking with Molly, Jonathan, and Portia Holman

learned to work together. At the end of each summer term they produced their own play. The children, as Dora explained, would agree on the general ideas of a plot, and then each would make up his or her lines. These, remember, were five- and six-year-olds. On one occasion a visitor said to one of the children, 'We hear you wrote your own play.' 'Oh, no, Mouse' (the name of the teacher) 'wrote it, but we told her what to put.'

One of the plays was called 'Thinking in front of yourself'. This has become something of a slogan in my life, and it is also the title of a splendid collection of the plays which Dora published with the Janus Press in 1934.

Needless to say, we devoted a great deal of time and thought to choosing the schools that were to come after Beacon Hill. We had a fascinating time visiting schools and interviewing headmasters; with our progressive ideas, conviction that children should not be dragooned into religion, and a growing feeling that a headmaster with too commanding a personality might cramp the development of the boys, however admirable he might be in other ways, we had a hard time making a choice. Eventually we settled on Bryanston. The school had been set up on what seemed highly progressive lines in the year Jeremy was born, though it was, by that time, becoming a little set in its ways. However, the boys were relaxed and happy and the headmaster, T.F. Coade, had many good ideas.

25. Jonathan and Jeremy with their mother in America in wartime

He was a sincere man and, although he was intensely religious, he did not believe in imposing his ideas on the pupil. The boys could decide for themselves.

The organization of school work was interesting. The boys were encouraged from the start to do a good deal of work on their own, and formal classes played a smaller and smaller part in the timetable as they went up through the school. Marking was not competitive, and there were no class lists; boys were marked against their own expected standard of performance. The classes were not organized in the usual way, with boys grouped in one class for all subjects. For each subject, the boys of any given year were divided into sets, so that they could work with the high-flyers in subjects where they showed ability, but go at an easier pace where they found difficulty.

So far as Jonathan was concerned, all our searching had little practical result; he was at Bryanston for only a short time when the war swept him off to the conventional Upper Canada College. Jeremy, however, came back from Canada and had three years at Bryanston. As we hoped, the school did prove to be an educational success, encouraging boys to develop their own ideas and abilities.

Looking back on the decisions we made, I am still satisfied that the choices we made were educationally good – although it is interesting that both the boys have decided to send their own children to much more conventional schools. They have also, incidentally, shown great hostility to intelligence testing, to which we attached considerable importance when they were young. However, we had not at that stage fully learned the importance of the family — a common mistake in the 1930s. I think we sent the boys to boarding school too early and did not give them enough of the family background that is so important in development.

This might have been the end of the story; but before Jeremy left school we were to have one more fascinating opportunity to put into practice the ideas we had developed about the importance of responsibility and decision-making for the young. This was the Theta club, a children's sailing club which is still flourishing nearly forty years after it was started. But as will be seen, this was not the result of any plan of ours.

Our own interest in sailing goes back a very long way. When I was stationed at Rosyth during the First World War, Captain Jones, the navigator of the *Lion*, used to take midshipmen sailing in the pinnace. With him I learned quite a lot. Molly's experience goes back even further. Already an enthusiast for model yachts, she had her first dinghy sailing at Thorpness on a family holiday in 1914. When our boys were quite young — perhaps three or four — we started taking half-deckers from Dick Southgate's yard in Horning, on the Norfolk Broads. The boys soon began to enjoy sailing, and Dick, who had a sixth sense and could sail a Broads cruiser against the tide among trees with hardly any wind, taught us a lot.

When we acquired the Martham Yard (see Chapter 19), it occurred to us that it would make an excellent place for children; camping in the dry shed and sailing the boats. We wrote a memorandum of our plans in 1944: an orthodox holiday camp run by adults for the young. Theta turned out very different.

The first holiday, in the spring of 1945, was a great success. There were ten or twelve children — boys from Bryanston and their sisters, three daughters of Hampstead friends, and some friends of Jonathan's. Everyone wanted to come again. During the summer, we bought our cottage in Thurne, and rented a barn for the children to sleep in. Again there were many there, and great enthusiasm. The children, who were becoming more competent, would go off sailing on their own; in the evening, they would come up to the cottage for supper and would sing part-songs — this singing, which was a great delight to us, was an important feature of club life for some years.

There were two important moments during this holiday. First, the children came up one day in the usual way to ask us where they should go and what they should buy for supper. Molly and I were busy with something else. Go away and decide for yourselves, we said. That was the beginning of self-government. And at the end of the holiday, we began to tot up what we had spent. It was more than we could afford. It began to seem that we would not be able to go on with our plans. However, the children had other ideas. Of course they would come again, they said. And why should we pay? They would form a club, and pay their own way. That winter there were long meetings in our flat in Lawn Road, while the details were settled and the club's long constitution drawn up.

At the beginning Molly and I were naturally assumed to be in charge and were appointed commodore and vice-commodore. It was obviously important to establish a high standard of competence in boat handling, and I had great fun setting exercises in sailing skill. Molly and I would go sailing with the children, and select those who seemed to us sufficiently competent to be given charge of a boat to be appointed as skippers.

It was not very long, though, before the skippers came to us and said that they were quite able to make their own selections for future skippers; and not long after that, the members protested that they too should have a say in the matter: a skipper must be somebody whose orders they were prepared to follow. They thus established a constitution in which candidate skippers were nominated by existing skippers and elected from this list by the ordinary members of the club. The discussion could be tough, and once or twice it ended in tears; but the members recognized from the start the importance of establishing high standards.

The selection of members was equally important. We had bought and converted an army landing-craft to be a headquarters for the club; it was fitted with bunks to sleep twelve, although on one occasion there were twenty-one aboard. In such confined quarters it was important that members should be sociable; so while potential new members were introduced by being invited as guests for a week, they too were subject to rigorous discussion afterwards before they were offered membership. Then there was the problem of chores. If everyone went sailing and the wind fell, they would all return in the dark to a mess, with no food, and great difficulty in getting anything done. They soon established a system of working parties, under which three of the group would stay behind every day to do the housework and make improvements around the Ark, as the landing-craft was now called.

As commodore, I was being more and more reduced to the role of chairman. One enjoyable ritual happened every Friday night. The whole party from the Ark would come up and spend the evening in our cottage and we would have a session of postmortems. The skipper in charge of any boat that had got into trouble (and there was never any shortage) was asked to describe the whole incident and how it had happened; his crew then told him where his account had gone wrong. Everyone then discussed what lessons could be drawn from the episode.

The members were learning more than just sailing and living harmoniously at close quarters. They took charge of their own finances, and learned some valuable lessons. At one stage the fee for a week's sailing, including food, was reduced to three and a half guineas; it was soon apparent that this left an inadequate fund for replacing worn-out equipment and maintaining boats, and the members voted unanimously to raise the fee again. They also had to learn to conduct their relations with the grown-up world outside. At one stage – and it tended to happen through the years – standards of smartness and discipline dropped very low. Hired boats were returned in poor condition, and late, and the boatyards (with a little covert encouragement from me) said they would not be willing to hire boats to the club any more. A deputation from the club spent a week in Norfolk, and succeeded in persuading the hirers to give them a second chance; and for a time the standards of smartness would have met the demands of the Royal Navy.

The membership was loyal and enthusiastic, and many of them spent almost their entire holidays with the club. As a result, a new problem arose after two or three years. The club, as one member put it at the meeting, was getting older at the rate of one year per annum. This meant both that there was a shortage of young recruits, and that some of the members who were still regularly coming were by now too old to be called children. The essence of the club – a place where children could run their own affairs – was in danger. There had also been some problems with young guests who found themselves under the charge of rather young skippers. At fifteen or sixteen, these skippers found the task of taking responsibility for incompetent eleven- or twelve-year-olds a bit too much for them.

26. Molly in her mid-twenties

After long discussion at the annual meeting, they found a solution which attacked both problems at once. The club would start so-called Infants' Weeks, at which children too young to be full members would be invited to come up for a week's holiday and training. This was more like the holiday camp we had once imagined. These weeks, it was clear, should preferably be run by those members who were still enthusiastic, but beginning to outgrow a children's club – they could still enjoy Theta without getting in the way. Election from infant to member was just as tough as election to skipper. Suitability for membership and some willingness to muck in was essential; if friends of elder brothers or sisters had to be offended, then so be it.

Gradually the powers of the commodore faded away until he was left with only one duty: if the club wanted to give someone the sack, the commodore would have to do it. This happened only once. There was a crisis when a couple of members – a boy and a girl – decided, against the orders of the senior skipper, to transfer their mattresses to a half-decker and sleep there, and not with the others.

This was a serious situation; one of the skippers at the time described it as agonizing. The unspoken law of the club was that living together, at close quarters, in the Ark explained why, as one member put it at the annual meeting, 'the Theta birth-rate is still zero'.

It was not for us to solve this problem. Instead, we invited the club committee – which by this time boasted a chairman, vice-chairman, secretary, treasurer, bosun and organizer – to come to supper. We ate comfortably in the Isobar – perhaps a little gin in the vermouth. It soon emerged that they were worried about the whole future of the club. If skippers were to be defied, the rules by which the club functioned were at risk. They were also afraid that if discipline over sleeping broke down, the club might get a bad name. This was not a matter of morality: members were welcome to behave as they liked – but not on a club session. Molly and I still refused to take any action. We learnt later that, as a result, the matter was discussed at great length at the next annual meeting. The committee recommended sacking. After much agonizing, the members agreed. The boy in question – who was rather unpopular anyway – resigned.

Just after the war, when the club was started, holiday opportunities for children were rather limited; it was perhaps easy to understand why members were so enthusiastic. It is, though, rather astonishing that the club has continued, long away from any influence of ours, for thirty years. The opportunities for children are now almost unlimited. Yet the club, sailing on the Norfolk Broads – which have become sadly less attractive over the years – and living in spartan quarters, has continued.

The reasons seem clear. Members, from the founding days to the present, have always told me that one of the strongest appeals of the club is that it is self-governing. The children enjoy sailing, certainly, but membership of something of their own, which they run themselves without interference, is something quite special. There have been problems from time to time, it is true. Boat maintenance is a persistent headache; at other times there have been outbreaks of not altogether friendly warfare with neighbouring scout camps, and episodes when the local pub landlord proved too ready to serve members who were well under age. All the same, the club has shown staying power. I think Bertie Russell and A.S.Neill would be pleased with this unconscious, voluntary tribute to their ideas.

9
Lawn Road Flats

The Lawn Road Flats building, designed by Wells Coates, was completed in July 1934. I sometimes wonder whether the Lawn Road Flats would ever have been built had I had the experience I have now, but with all the stupid mistakes I made I am very glad we took the plunge.

Molly and I had planned to have a house built for ourselves and land had been bought in Lawn Road. We asked Molly's sister, Jill, and her husband, Harry Harrison, to design it.

We had not yet learnt the importance of the 'brief'. Harry made a first sketch. It was of a charming little neo-Georgian house that gave a nod to the modern. It was white amongst the trees, with corner windows. The drawing was shown at the Royal Academy.

Jill and Harry were good practical architects brought up at the AA, where the dominant personalities were Howard Robertson, Robert Atkinson and Goodhart-Rendel, but they remained close to the Georgian tradition.

I had first met Wells Coates, as I explained before, during my Venesta period, when he was designing interiors for Cresta. Wells had a powerful personality. He was passionately sincere in his designing, but sometimes in his hurry and anxiety to achieve an objective he would give a false impression of superficiality. Molly's strong liking for him proved fortunate, since she was able to deal with his sometimes strange behaviour: he was very difficult at times.

Very soon we decided to ask Wells Coates to design our house instead of Jill and Harry. When he showed us his design we were bowled over straight away and said so.

There were hardly any points to raise for alteration or adjustment, but foolishly I asked about waste disposal. Wells was furious, nearly tearing up the plans. How could we discuss his plans on the same level as dustbins? Fortunately, Molly was able to calm him down.

Beatrix Tudor Hart was running a successful little nursery school on the top floor of our house in Platts Lane. It seemed logical to consider including a nursery school on our land. Wells jumped at the idea and started new drawings to include one small infant school.

During our discussions with Wells, Molly said that she supposed that really land in London should be used for more than one family. Wells, in one of his superior moods, said, 'Of course, I always knew that the right thing to do was to build flats rather than a house.' Anthony Jackson in his book *Politics of Architecture* says that it was Wells who persuaded us, but the decision was much more the product of a general discussion amongst the three of us, although it was Wells who kept up the pressure. But where was the money to build flats to come from?

We decided to have a go at raising the money. Molly drew up a splendid brief. She described the kind of people we thought the building should be for: they would be young professional men and women with few possessions. They would have an income of around £500 a year. Molly described their requirements, for sleeping, cooking, eating, storage of clothes and other simple needs. She also described the minimum domestic service that would be required: window-cleaning, dusting, bed-making. We also offered simple meals to be supplied by a manager. Our own flat was planned for the roof of the building, only to be completed as and when we could afford it. The brief said nothing about size, shape or design – that was up to the architect.

Our ideas – political, architectural and personal – were developing and we were changing fast. Working at Venesta had brought me into contact with the ideas of Walter Gropius and the Bauhaus, with their emphasis on ways to improve the mechanics of living. Le Corbusier had proposed a living space without doors, privacy of a kind being provided by ingenious planning. Wells's solution was even simpler. However, when the plans were approved and put out for estimating, even the lowest estimate was a good deal too high for our resources.

I suggested we should have an easy, open, friendly discussion with Wells and the builder to see if we might find and agree on some reduction in the cost. Wells did not like the idea. The meeting was a failure. It was always the same when there was even the smallest chance that his ability might be questioned. He had to be infallible.

Of course, we had to go ahead after all. Wells's plans were so very good. I was bewildered and hardly dared think about what we were undertaking.

A company had been formed in December 1931. Wells often used isometric perspective in his drawings, and the Lawn Road Flats were in a form of modular units, so 'Isometric Unit Construction' soon became Isokon – not Isaacs and Cohen, as some have suggested.

Amongst the many architects I met at this time was Max Fry, who was also a close friend of Wells's. Max was then involved with the Design and Industries Association, promoting an exhibition of industrial art at Dorland Hall, and it was proposed that the exhibition should contain a full-scale model of one of the Isokon minimum flats. It was a fine idea and most opportune. It would give the much-needed publicity to find tenants, although initially we would of course require more money.

The Dorland Hall exhibition was a great success, and although no building work had started we let twelve Lawn Road flats with deposits paid.

We were introduced to a firm of solicitors acting for financiers who were prepared to advance building finance at about $7\frac{1}{2}$ per cent (a high rate for those days) provided we put up £5,000, which was just about all Molly and I could find between us. The estimate for the building was £18,000.

27. Wells Coates: isometric drawing of Lawn Road Flats, Hampstead

ISOKON FLATS

We were to provide certificates each fortnight for work done, allowing us to then draw out £2,000. But each fortnight the lenders seemed to be adding extras. We had no experience in these matters and felt caught.

Fortunately, a remarkable accident saved the situation. Through John Gloag, I had become a member of the Design and Industries Association; what is more, I had recently been made chairman, and I had on my committee the great Frank Pick and, in spite of his importance as the General Manager of London Transport, he was easy and approachable.

I told him of my financial predicament, and he in the kindest way possible told me I was a silly young fool and that I must get rid of the lenders

28. Early advertisement for Lawn Road Flats

as soon as I could. Of course I acted too hastily, told them I wanted no more of their money and that I would repay what they had lent in the next fortnight. We had just fourteen days to find the money and no idea where it might come from.

With amazing good fortune I was introduced to McDonald, the manager of the District Bank in Waterloo Place. At first he said much the same as Frank Pick and also pointed out that the country had hardly got out of one of its worst financial crises, flats were empty, etc. When I told him I had deposits paid for twelve of the thirty flats he was amazed and came with me to Hampstead to see if the building was really under construction.

The result was that not only did we get the money we needed, but now it was to be at the ordinary bank rate.

All the time that we were having the flats built I was fortunately in my full-time job with Venesta. They knew what I was up to; they had seen the full-size model flat at the Dorland Hall Exhibition. They had made no protest.

Our specifications for the flats included various types of plywood. At Venesta we had set up a Building Uses Department. This brought me in touch with many architects and designers, which helped to sell Venesta plywood and encourage new uses — I was beginning to be known. I once received a letter addressed to 'Plywood Pritchard London'!

There was some delay in getting the building started. I had assumed that permission from the LCC would come in the form of a definite statement, 'yes' or 'no', but their letter referred to no particular objections. At the time this vagueness was disconcerting. I learnt later that that letter could be taken as approval. Wells kept on saying get on with it, I held back, trying to get a firm OK. The result was that, instead of the concreting being completed before the cold weather, the delay meant waiting till the following spring.

While the building was in progress I was sent by Venesta to France. Once when travelling south with E.A.Gruenberg, the managing director of Luterna Français, I took a Saturday and Sunday off to visit Montague Napier. Molly's father was on the board of Napier Motors, and I had been invited to go and call on him if ever my work took me to Nice, where he kept his large yacht. I was given a suite of rooms with bath. Meals were brought to me. I lived those two days in great luxury on board his yacht. I then went on to Marseilles with Gruenberg. There I found a letter from the Hampstead Borough Council. It had been forwarded from Hampstead to me at Venesta, who had sent it on to Paris, from where it had come to Marseilles. The letter was a request that I should quickly remove a couple of trees from our land in Lawn Road that had fallen across the road and were holding up the traffic!

Meanwhile the flats in Lawn Road progressed. We were proud of them. Visitors began to have a look. One was an old lady whom I had noticed on more than one occasion; she would stop for a moment and then go on. I asked her if she liked the building. No, she said, she hated it, but somehow it always had such a nice atmosphere and she wondered why. She added, 'Why have such small windows?' I explained that the building was placed at an angle to the road, that the small windows were for the kitchens and would face north-east and keep cool, and the sitting rooms were on the other side, with large windows facing south-west to get the sun. She said she had never considered such a thing and thought it a wonderful idea. She hastened to say with a happy smile that she still hated the building but liked walking by it.

There was another visitor, a well-known architect who came in with an assistant and a measuring rod. They came as if not wanting to be observed. It happened that I saw them. I collected a roll of drawings and went down and suggested that it would be simpler if they had the drawings and would they please return them when they had finished with them.

We had a grand opening. H. de C. Hastings of the *Architectural Review* said that if he could have exclusive rights, he would print an article on the concept of the building, to be written by Molly. Unfortunately – or the reverse – many other papers came to report and take photographs, and so Molly's article, which would have included her original brief to Wells Coates, was never published; but other very good articles were.

Thelma Cazalet, MP, formally opened the building on 9 July 1934. It was probably the first, or almost the first, of the so-called modern buildings in Britain. Others built at much the same time were Lubetkin's Highpoint in Highgate and Gibberd's Pullman Court in Streatham. Connell, Ward and Lucas's High and Over was a year or so earlier.

David Embling wrote in December 1947 that the building was a pioneering experiment in the use of monolithic reinforced concrete. Apart from the beams, the concrete was four inches thick with an inch of cork to provide insulation and, because the main-line railway tunnels from St Pancras ran under Lawn Road, it was necessary for a cantilever to be constructed over the tunnels at each end of the building.

In each small kitchen was a cooker, refrigerator and storage space. There

29. Thelma Cazalet opening the Flats, watched by the Pritchard family (my mother on far right), in 1934

was also a dressing-room with fitted cupboards and wash-basin. The bathroom and lavatory led out of the dressing-room. The twenty-two single flats had a sitting-room with a sliding table, single bedstead and mattress. In the double flats, there was a round table and a large bed. It is not the act of sleeping in a room that tends to make bedsitters disagreeable; it is the accumulation of domestic things – clothing and so on. Wells surmounted this problem by providing storage facilities; so much convenience in such a small space.

Wells provided for a service lift and a small pantry on each floor; the lift went up to the top floor and ended in our small kitchen. On each of the floors there were service trolleys with electric hot-plates. These trolleys fitted into the small pantries. Each flat had a telephone to the central kitchen.

Flat 1 was to be set aside for a resident housekeeper, her job being to supervise the cleaning staff and, when called on, to supply meals to tenants' flats. The arrangements for staff were ample: a large kitchen with a pantry which provided some space for resting as well as space

30. Opening day at Lawn Road Flats, with guests along the roof-line

for food storage and a small laundry, and a staff sitting-room not much smaller than the size of a standard single flat.

We overestimated the demand for meals, tenants preferring to use their efficient little kitchens. Later my daughter, Jennifer, designed a simple fitment that could go into the three single flats without kitchens – flats originally planned for short stay tenants who, as we discovered, very often stayed on permanently. Jennifer's fitment had a hot-plate, refrigerator and sink: very neat and convenient.

There were always fairly regular requests from schools of architecture, art and design, to see over the building and the furniture in our own flat. The first visit was from Sweden. The DIA had suggested that the Lawn Road Flats were one of the sights to see in London. The Swedish party was organized by the Svenska Slojdforeningen. Gregor Paulsson was director. He was soon to be Professor of Fine Art at Uppsala.

The last visit was forty-one years later, in 1976. Besides a dozen students from the Architectural Association, it was particularly good that Hugh Casson and Max Fry came as well. Both knew Wells and the building from its pre-natal days.

Then there were the tenants; on the whole they were a distinguished lot. The first to sleep in the building were Lella and Professor Philip Sargent Florence. They were in No. 6, the downstairs double at the south end; they were not permanent tenants, just temporary visitors for a night or two. The building was still being completed. Other early tenants included Gathorne Hardy, Miss McMichael, secretary to Handley Page, and Kenneth Robinson, one of the best Ministers of Health and later Chairman of the Arts Council, when his intervention at the time of the 'Thirties' exhibition at the Hayward was to prove so useful to us.

There was, of course, Walter Gropius, who came here from Nazi Germany in October 1934 and stayed until he went to Harvard in 1937. (His time in England is described in the next chapter.) Marcel Breuer, Moholy-Nagy, Arthur Korn, Jacques and Jacqueline Groag, Diana and Kenneth Rowntree (he was later Professor of Fine Art in Newcastle, while Diana wrote on architecture in the *Guardian*); Agatha Christie and her husband, Professor Max Mallowan. Nicholas Monsarrat was there for a short time at the beginning. Montgomery Belgion stayed quite a long time and while there wrote his book on France, which was published just before the war. Edmund Kapp made a lithograph of me in lieu of rent. I was not allowed to see the drawing until it was finished; one Sunday Polly Hill had a look. 'It's just like him,' she said, 'not particularly flattering.' Later he had an exhibition in the Isobar. Michael Gould had his first show in the Isobar.

W.J.Brown, another tenant, later helped to persuade the Government

31. Lawn Road Flats: the east side of Wells Coates's building

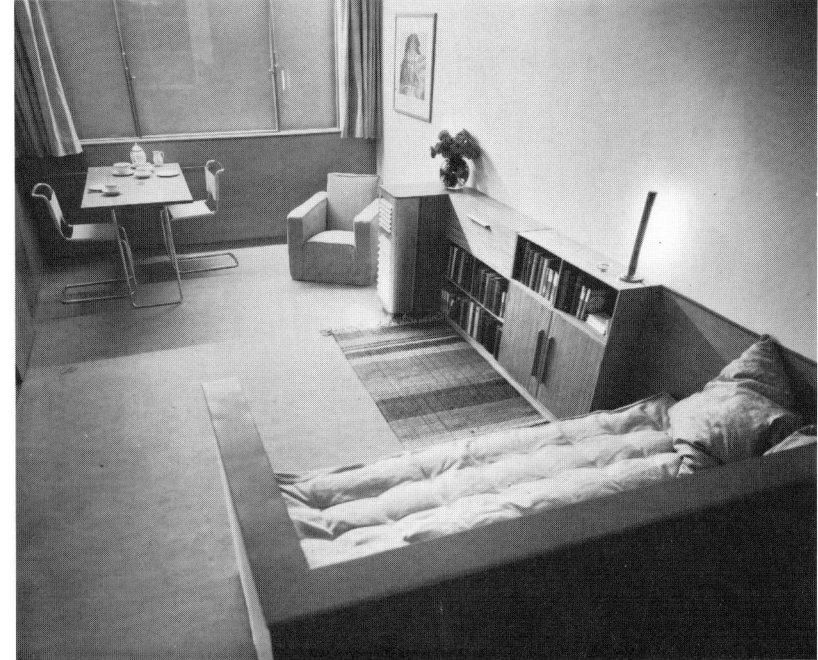

32. No. 6, Lawn Road Flats: all-purpose living-room with sliding door through to dressing-room and bathroom
33. Wells Coates's Minimum Flat as originally shown at Dorland Hall in 1933

34. Lawn Road Flats: standard kitchen with built-in fitments
35. Standard dressing-room
36. No. 15, the flat allotted to Walter and Ise Gropius when they arrived in England

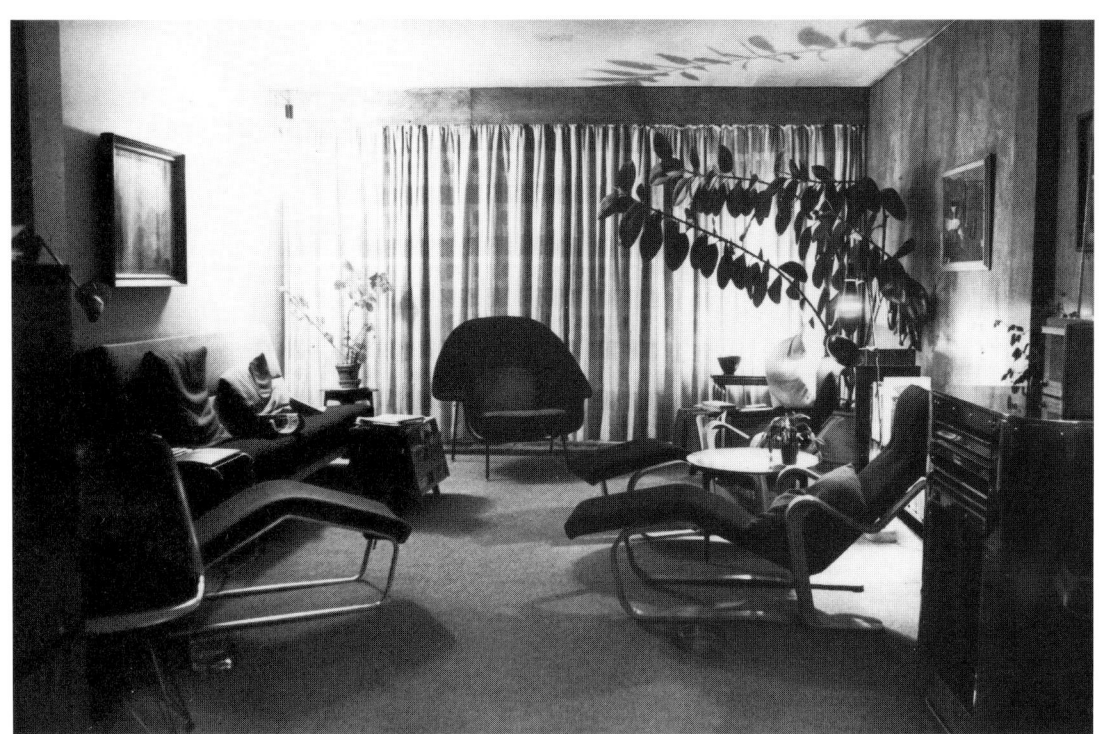

37. The Pritchards' flat at Lawn Road. Wells Coates's electric fire in copper Plymax is in the foreground

to publish the report on domestic heating in America that I, and two others, had written towards the end of the war for the Ministry of Fuel and Power.

Professor Gordon Childe was also very good value. He had a very large American car, a Terraplane, that sometimes got in the way of others of moderate size. He was a brilliant archaeologist and one of the very few members of the Communist Party I had met who had a strong sense of humour and wit. One evening in the Club when the Party was in some muddle I asked him his opinion. He looked up, with his fine runcible nose and a smile. 'I don't know, I have not yet read the *Daily Worker*,' he said, and laughed.

Other residents, at one time or another, included Professor Hilary Marquand, who was Minister of Health in the post-war Labour Government, Charles Madge, Sir Harry Campion, the head of the Government Central Statistical Office, Professor S.R.K.Granville, and for a few weeks, Irina and Henry Moore.

There was a young dentist who was starting his new practice. He was finding difficulty in getting his car out because of someone parking clumsily. He was obviously in a bit of a state. I said that if he would be patient for a moment I thought I could help. 'I can be patient,' he said, 'but I only have one and I am late for him already.'

Graham Maw, a friend from Cambridge, who was our solicitor, devised a standard lease. We took considerable trouble over the typography and got away from the normal stodgy format. The lease was divided into two sections – the lease proper and a codicil that summarized what the landlord would endeavour to undertake for the tenants and the rules that the tenant would be bound to.

When we were promoting the flats we never gave a thought to their management. The idea of the building was the thing that mattered. Management could look after itself. But as the building went up we began to worry, and asked Mim Gloag, John's wife, a sensible and practical person, to advise us. She helped us to get our first manageress, and Molly and I assumed that we need have no further worries.

When the manageress had to leave, we found a new one. She was unsatisfactory and soon left. The problem then was to find a suitable manager to whom we could delegate the management and yet keep a close hand on the finances.

In the early days before Molly wrote her brief we considered a restaurant, and thought that it should be on the roof with a terrace. We were persuaded against this by Robert Spicer, whom I met during the PEP and Techplan meetings and who was on our board. He was then working for a large departmental store and his reports on the problems of its catering activities deterred us.

We were, however, already much involved with the movement for improving standards of food in England. The 'Half Hundred' dining club was founded by Philip Harben, Raymond Postgate and Molly and me. André Simon's Wine and Food Society was too large, too expensive and too pompous. We wanted it the other way round.

For the Half Hundred we had a price limit for food, for wine and overheads; we stipulated that conversation was to be free of taboos, and members should be members in their own right and not be brought in as a wife or husband.

Raymond Postgate drafted the rules, the first of which were as follows:

1. The Club shall be known as the Half Hundred and shall consist of not more than twenty-five members, each of whom shall have the right to bring one guest. The object of the Club is to combine good dining with economy.
2. Members other than foundation members must be proposed and seconded by existing members. No member may propose his or her wife or husband and no candidate shall be proposed who has not previously attended at least one dinner as guest. Members must be elected nem. con. and a member proposing a candidate must certify him or her to be seriously and intelligently interested in food and drink and to possess no religious or other taboos or unsociable charac-

teristics which may impede conversation. No person wholly or principally employed in the wine or food trade shall be eligible for membership, but existing members who enter these trades shall not be asked to resign.

Members were called on by rota to direct or cook the dinners. Those attending would pay not more than ten shillings a head. This was made up of food at two shillings and sixpence, wine at five shillings, and two shillings and sixpence for cooking and service, etc. If the director spent more, that was his business. Most of the dinners kept close to the cost allowance and were very good. A minority of meals were just extravaganzas, bringing their director no kudos only extra expense – for members would only pay the regulation ten shillings. There were many interesting and amusing meals, everyone taking pride in what he or she produced.

Meetings of the Half Hundred were usually held in our flat. The dinners were sometimes cooked there in our tiny kitchen; some members brought dishes already prepared. Later, when the Isobar was founded, meals for the Half Hundred were cooked in the Isobar kitchen and sent up to our flat.

The Isobar was started when we asked Breuer to design the conversion of the over-sized kitchen provided for the flat on the ground floor into a club restaurant.

He made a splendid arrangement. We called it the Isobar because Molly was interested in weather. A barograph was put at one end of the Club Room. Breuer made a feature of it, showing its works behind a large piece of glass about a foot high, curved back at each side with a photograph of clouds behind. The total width, about two feet, looked fine, and the daily recordings from the barograph were kept. At the other end of the room was the bar, so that should members find their pressure low they could get it raised at the bar.

The first choice of manager for the Club was Tommy Layton. That was not satisfactory, so Philip Harben took over and ran the Isobar. He and his wife, Kathy, became the managers of the building as well. The atmosphere changed at once.

The Isobar began attracting more members and their friends; there were artists, designers, critics, statisticians and architects: Ben Nicholson, Barbara Hepworth, Jim Richards, Wells Coates, Serge Chermayeff and others. One delightful episode which took place soon after the Isobar opened was the reunion of Gabo and Slutzky. They met there for the first time after leaving Russia. They were both small men. They rushed towards each other and embraced with such delight that all in the Club were entranced.

38. The Isobar designed by Marcel Breuer during his residency at Lawn Road, 1935–6
39. Philip Harben fondue-making. He ran the Isobar in the late 1930s, before he came to fame as the first television cook
40. A corner of the dining area in the Isobar, with Breuer's plywood tables, matched with stools from Estonia

Philip and Kathy Harben remained with us for a part of the war. They were doing a wonderful job. Philip's cooking was fascinating. The change from peace to war produced new problems that at first were hardly recognized: tenants were losing their jobs, or trying to get out of London. It was not a sudden change, but soon we had many difficulties. We continued to insist on our three-year leases when, with hindsight, we should have been more flexible.

As the war went on, those who had to work in London began to appreciate the fact that the flats were built of reinforced concrete. Tenants began to come back. We were determined to keep the service going as long as possible and succeeded throughout the war. Philip was called up to join the RAF in June 1940; I heard that his job was to solve the problem of providing Winston Churchill with hot coffee and boiled eggs when flying high without a pressurized cabin.

Within days of Philip's departure Robert Braun arrived. I had known Robert since 1927. He was working for my brother's advertising agency and saw me at Venesta. Not long before the war he had been running a little shop in Paris.

As the Nazis were approaching Paris his French cousin offered him a large car with an immense quantity of money if he would drive a couple of elderly aunts to Bordeaux, buy them a house and get them settled in. He could have what was left. He later wrote how he left Paris 'in a haze of smoke', travelled to Bayonne and then to Bordeaux. He described how sometimes he had to drive over fields, and through machine-gun fire, but he successfully deposited the aunts in a small house outside Bordeaux, left them all the money and managed to get a boat to Falmouth. He came straight to the Lawn Road Flats, and was without money or job.

Years later he wrote: 'You were my first call in London . . . your Austrian porter interned . . . Philip Harben in the RAF . . . would I come and fill the gap?' That's just what he did.

Robert was splendid. He built on what the Harbens had established. He started up a series of special dinners and he did well in reletting vacant flats.

The Isobar became the only restaurant in London where bananas and cream could be served in wartime (the banana had become extinct). Robert first bought up an old stock of tinned cream, then went round Soho buying packets of dried bananas and so made 'bananas and cream'.

During the early part of the war, while Molly was still in America, lemons were already in short supply, so she asked a young American who was coming to London to bring me two or three lemons. He came and stop-

41. Molly with the Isokon craftsman Harry Mansell setting off on a tandem from Lawn Road Flats to ride to Esher

ped to dinner in the Club and, during dinner, he produced the lemons. There was a dead silence. He was taken aback and said, 'Oh, if I had known there was such a shortage I would have brought a case – I thought the two or three were just a joke.'

While Henry Moore was doing his air-raid shelter drawings he sometimes came to rest in my flat. He and I squeezed one of the lemons into liqueur glasses and solemnly drank the precious juice.

There were some strange scenes in the Isobar in wartime. During the Blitz some tenants brought down their bedding, preferring to sleep in the Club rather than high in the flats. It became quite a custom, some claiming a particular patch as their own. This conflicted with those who were dancing – and guests were inclined to want to stay too.

When Robert Braun had to leave, we were introduced to Lena Newman. She came as manageress and stayed with us for fifteen years, becoming almost one of the family. Lena remained with us until she was sixty – that would be in about 1951.

Meanwhile Maria had come on the scene, soon to become Jonathan's wife. She had come to England from Czechoslovakia. Her father had died many years before, and as the war approached, her mother managed to get Maria out of the country, while she herself stayed behind with her son to look after elderly relatives. She died in a concentration camp, but Freddie survived and came to England later.

Maria was trained by Lena to take over the running of the flats, and she became a very successful manager.

After the war, at the time of the Festival of Britain, Walter and Ise Gropius came back to England. They found London 'a jewel of a city' and more full of vitality than they had known it before, and they wrote about their early stay:

> Our arrival in the fall of 1934 in London and our subsequent stay for two and a half years in one of the apartments of Lawn Road Flats marked an entirely new chapter in our life and it is hard to think of any shelter in London that would have made us quite as happy. After having experienced an initial success of Modern Architecture in Germany we had been forced to leave everything in the destructive hands of Nazism and at this moment of defeat, it was of inestimable value to us to become right away part of a bold venture in the English architectural development. We cherished the privilege to be among the first to explore the features of this radically new attempt at apartment building. We loved the sociability of the whole lay-out, the honest unpretentiousness of the exterior and the excellently planned flats.

Paul Reilly was a tenant twice. He had worked with me at Venesta and became a tenant some time after we had both left the firm. Once when he left the building he wrote:

> After nearly a year's tenancy I should like to tell you how pleased I am with the place and with the service given. In my opinion a single flat here is the ideal home for a single person living in London. I am very thankful I decided to move in; my friends said I would find a modern concrete block noisy. If it is, I must be deaf.

Just before the war, Kenneth and Diana Rowntree held their wedding party at Lawn Road Flats. Years later, Diana wrote:

> We held our wedding reception on the timber deck outside the Isobar, on a sunny Saturday the first week of the war. Philip Harben kindly undertook to cook our wedding luncheon. The fowl he boiled for us was the first of so very many gastronomic treats I have failed to appreciate, but this did nothing to lessen the total contentment of the occasion and its setting. The wedding had been secular, our clothes were informal, and there was nowhere in the world I would rather have been that day. From our own reception we went to James Cubitt's reception, and I felt sorry for any couple who had to have their party indoors, even in an elegant Bloomsbury drawing-room.
>
> It was the blitz that finally admitted us to the heady, rational joys of Lawn Road Flats. In 1939 the rents were well above the income level of a twenty-four-year-old painter, supporting himself by sales of paintings, and a newly qualified architect. However, when the blast from a nearby bomb broke the windows of a top flat and frightened away its occupants we were offered the flat, without service, for £1.10. a week, which suited a £4.0. wage packet. After five years of developing a functional design philosophy at the drawing board, and by the dialectic of the A.A. Studios, to find oneself living in a flat designed according to those principles was indeed to come home.

No. 31 Lawn Road Flats performed entirely to our satisfaction, as Kenneth's studio by day, as a hospitable dining room by night, finally as bedroom luxuriously accoutred with a 6'0 long bath, spacious built-in dressing table and the dressing room I still remember with affection.

We only used the restaurant for special occasions, but the bar itself we frequented as much for the intoxicating cool of the intellects gathered there as of the beverages. While J.C.Pritchard was building his formidable palate, I was painstakingly acquiring the taste for draught beer.

This pure, twentieth century existence lasted less than a year. With the onset of our firstborn we felt it our duty to move into the country away from the bombs. It was twenty-nine years before we found another so congenial machine for living in.

Another ex-tenant wrote:

I certainly was a very contented inhabitant of Lawn Road Flats and couldn't possibly object to your saying so! My chief memories are of the fascination of finding a place where like the wood in *Dear Brutus*, trees really seemed to have moved close up to the windows. That, meals in the garden, and one particularly beautiful white blossoming cherry tree are the things I have never forgotten. The social side of life I have always been bad at and seldom remember! But places make their mark. Coming up the street the flats looked just like a giant liner which ought to have had a couple of funnels, and then you went up the stairs and through the door of one's flat and there were the trees tapping on the window.

That was Agatha Christie.

Breuer wrote from America on the occasion of the building's coming of age:

It is good to know that Lawn Road Flats will have a birthday, just like any other human being. I always liked that girl, and I think she is getting younger from year to year. She is a generous wench, a friendly and hospitable one – not too careful with what she has. I wish all pretty girls were the same . . . I'm sure you agree! In other words, let me send this note off as a birthday card for Lawn Road Flats and if it sounds a bit nostalgic it is only because it reminds me that already nineteen years have passed since I lived with her.

On 14 July 1955, we had a twenty-first birthday party for the building. It was a happy occasion. Nikolaus Pevsner and Henry Morris made short speeches. Pevsner, of course, put the building into the context of its time:

So as regards architecture proper, and especially domestic architecture, it was really only at the end of 1933, when the Dorland Hall Exhibition was on, that the change began. There one heard for the first time of a mysterious block of flats that was to go up in Hampstead and was to show London what the new style in the domestic field was really about. In 1934 the building was ready – Jack Pritchard Act two – and now we are standing in it – with Wells Coates, whose after-life as long as architectural historians will busy themselves with English architecture is at once secured. It was sure enough a milestone – it looks too as if it were built of milestones.

> Now you must allow me to say that the Lawn Road Flats looked at in 1955 are extremely dated, and they are extremely dated because they are giant's work of the 1930s.
>
> It was a manifesto and I suppose that, after the novelty of any building has worn off and before the patina comes out, there can be nothing as important for a building than to be a manifesto. The gist of the manifesto in this case, and I think it is wholly valid, is to get down to the essentials of living without compromises with convention. Very well, if one formulates it like that, I suppose that applies as much to the living programme of Lawn Road as it does to the appearance.

Henry Morris said:

> The distinguishing mark of Lawn Road over the twenty-one years it has been in existence, is that it has been a kind of society and that it had something of a corporate character. I don't think that can be said of any other block of flats in London or in England, and it's a great achievement.

He continued:

> When Lawn Road began, for a long time there were a number of people here from the most varied walks of life – administration, science and the universities, painters and writers. It was a most agreeable society, many of the people doing work of interest and importance, and they knew each other. That was one element.

Then, referring to the Club, he said:

> Then next, there was this Club room and the dining room. I remember how for a long time until the middle of the war one could come to Lawn Road and dine sometimes subtly and always wholesomely for a very small sum indeed.
>
> Then also there was the social side to it with a kind of Common Room to which people could always go. It was extremely agreeable. I also noted too, that there were people who lived at Lawn Road and people who came and stayed here like myself. And I used to see frequently men and women who had left the place for many years and gone abroad who, coming back to London and feeling rather at a loss, would make straight for Lawn Road and find what they wanted, friends and that most attractive atmosphere.

Henry Morris wound up with:

> I would like to end by saying that I hope that those two people, Jack Pritchard and Molly Pritchard, who were, if I may say so, the originating and presiding geniuses over this establishment, will see to it that in the near future something of that essential spirit of the place will be recaptured and will go on.

The sale of Lawn Road Flats

We decided to sell Lawn Road Flats so we could be free of the responsibility of the burden of finding ways to deal with the maintenance. It was also a chance for both Molly and me and the boys to gain some capital.

At the end of January 1968 I went to see Richard Llewelyn-Davies, the architect and planner, to ask if he knew of any institution that would be likely to be interested in taking over the flats and, as a result, we were approached by a hospital. The idea was to use the building for senior nursing staff and junior doctors. The Club would be kept and used not only for the new tenants but for other hospital staff in the neighbourhood. It seemed perfect. Unfortunately, after six months of negotiation with the hospital's agent, we were told they did not want to buy the flats after all.

When, then, the *New Statesman and Nation* people expressed interest we considered them to be a good second choice. We believed, wrongly as it turned out, that they would be a suitable body to care for a building that was regarded as having both social and architectural merit and that they would be interested in its history. They thought it might be used to house visiting professors and others.

I lunched with Kingsley Martin, Gerald Barry and Jeremy Potter in the Isobar, and they then expressed great pleasure at being able to take over and preserve the building, although Potter's enthusiasm was rather less than that of the other two. It was only after the agreement was signed that I realized fully that these buyers had no real interest in the building's social and historic importance and that it had been purchased simply as a profitable investment.

We had offered the building to the hospital at as low a figure as we could in view of the social use to which the building was to be put, and we stupidly offered it to the *New Statesman* at the same figure – a gross mistake. A valuation had been extremely difficult to arrive at, since it involved not only revenues from the rents of the flats but also an assessment of their potential; we knew there were landlords who could make the place more profitable, but we valued the social life of the Club and the other aspects that were not 'profitable'. Eventually we sold for £70,000. Three years later the building was sold to the Camden Borough Council for £150,000. This big difference was caused first by my mishandling of the valuation and also by the considerable outlay which proved to be needed for renovation. We stayed on in the flat for some time after the Camden Borough Council took over the building. In some ways they were very good landlords.

At the time of the take-over, there was a great meeting in our flat. Present were Corin Hughes-Stanton, Chairman of the Housing Committee, William Barnes, Director of Housing, his assistant, H.A.Hunt, and one or two others. Corin, who was editor of *Design* magazine, explained that he wanted the building preserved in a responsible way; the structure would be maintained under the supervision of the Architects Department of the Council, and the Housing Department would be responsible for its management.

Under our administration the tenants were provided with a well-defined domestic service that included bed-making, dusting and window-cleaning, the taking away of refuse and receiving parcels.

Camden agreed to maintain the service for existing tenants only, for a charge of £2 per week, and not for the new council tenants. I had wished that the Council would make an experiment with our building and provide some minimum service for old people, the plans of the flats being particularly suitable for this use.

When Corin Hughes-Stanton was no longer Chairman of the Housing Committee, it became increasingly clear that the established administration, while giving courteous acknowledgment to the elected representatives of the people, went on their own sweet way.

There are three examples of the lack of architectural understanding by the Housing Department. In No. 31, where our children lived, the floor was the same as in our flat: thick plywood and insulation with an eighth of an inch of plywood on the surface. This had proved entirely satisfactory, but when some new wiring had to be installed the men doing the preparatory work had never met a plywood floor and, before any protest could be made, they ripped it up and put down planks – a quite unnecessary expense.

Then there were the ventilating glass bricks in the staircase. Wells had left regular apertures up the stair column of about 9 inches by 4 inches with three pieces of thick glass placed in such a way as to provide thin gaps for ventilation. The Housing Department painted over the bricks so that there was no ventilation.

When the Council put in a fine new heating installation it had to occupy the whole of the garage space, and in order to get ventilation they broke through the reinforced concrete outer wall, thus spoiling the façade. With a little architectural understanding, the ventilation could have been provided elsewhere.

The Housing Department suggested as a normal practice that there should be a tenants' committee. On the whole it worked well. There was, however, one unfortunate episode.

The building had by then become a 'listed building'. As such it should have been preserved in a condition as near as possible to its original one. When the building needed repainting, for some reason the Council resented being told by us that the original colour had been white with a very faint suggestion of pink. So they decided to consult the tenants' committee. Would they prefer the building to be painted white or pink? Of course the reply was 'white'. It looked reasonably well, but without the subtlety of a hint of pink.

A replica of an Isokon Minimum Flat was shown at the 'Thirties' exhibition at the Hayward Gallery in 1979. The original idea of Neave Brown, the architect for the exhibition, was to make the flat a throughway. This, of course, would have destroyed the essential completeness of Wells Coates's design. Those visitors who were not aware of the original plans would have walked through and on one side would have been a well designed kitchen, a neat dressing-room and a bathroom with the lavatory, and on the other side unit furniture; they would not have appreciated the unity of the whole.

It was hard to find who was responsible for the decision, so we wrote to all and sundry including the Chairman of the Arts Council. Kenneth Robinson saw the point immediately – he had, as I mentioned, been a tenant at Lawn Road!

In the event, the flat was shown with little reference to the building; it was bitty and cold, lacking the character of the original flat shown at Dorland Hall in 1934. Apart from that, there was no lavatory pan, and they played music which they thought was typical 1930s. It was certainly not the music that tenants at Lawn Road would have played during the 1930s.

We had been proud to feel that one of the Lawn Road Flats was to be shown, but since it was so poorly exhibited perhaps it would have been better not to have been shown at all.

The Hayward exhibition gave the impression of being arranged by a committee rather than by an overall administrator who, in Henry Morris's definition, should be a thinker and a scholar who understood.

All the same I enjoyed it. It raised so many happy memories, but I was not thrilled as I had been in Sheffield where Fiona and David Mellor had put on 'A Century of British Design 1880–1980' at the Mappin Gallery.

10
Walter Gropius

When I met Henry Morris I had just left the Navy, and was young and immature. Cambridge seemed like an ever-expanding universe, and Henry the chief prophet. It was not long before I became one of his most enthusiastic and loving disciples. But by the time I met Gropius, I was more adult. Although Henry and Walter had very different origins, Henry's father having been a small builder and Walter's parents professional and well-established, they had developed many similar ideas.

The good fortune in working with Gropius has been one of the most important things in my life. There were five episodes: arranging with

Max Fry to get him out of Nazi Germany to Britain; trying to promote three building projects with him; his involvement with the Isokon Furniture Company; the building of Impington Village College with Henry Morris; and finally, much later in the 1970s, helping to get the travelling exhibition of his architecture to Britain.

In June 1934, I first met him for a brief moment at the Royal Institute of British Architects exhibition of his works, and I heard him give his paper to the Design and Industries Association, described by Max Fry.

'I can remember exactly', Max wrote, 'the overcrowded room and his standing amongst us, speaking with the utmost clarity in broken English on how we could mend the disunity of our machine civilization, and what moved us was the mixture of humility and authority with which he addressed us.' Max went on, 'He gave us in that moment an unexpected accession of strength and assurance. The theme was already familiar but not the depth of purpose with which he invested it.'

This was for me, and for Max, the beginning of a new adventure. Here was the powerful father figure, appearing at first formidable and silent. I was to find his humour and joy in life later.

Morton Shand, who knew the dangers that were gathering round him in Nazi Germany, encouraged Max and me to help Walter Gropius to come to England. Max provided a partnership and Isokon provided a flat with subsistence in the almost completed Lawn Road Flats.

At that time I did not know that he had married again and, at Victoria Station on 18 October 1934, out of the train came not only Walter but Ise. Ise told me later how Gropius had been invited to go to Italy to give a paper on his plans for the total theatre. Nazi Germany and Fascist Italy were allies, and it was not difficult to get a return ticket to Rome and back to Berlin. Once in Italy she found it easy to get their tickets adjusted to go home via London.

Of course I had arranged a single flat for Walter, and now I had to do something fast. I had a hurried conversation with Max and telephoned Molly to find some way of changing the single flat to a double – not so simple as we were short of furniture.

For their first weekend, they said they would like to see Stonehenge. As we drove west, we passed large hoardings on the roadside. One read, 'You are now entering the strong country.' I noticed that Ise whispered to Walter. A little further on there was another, which read simply, 'Take Courage.' Walter asked me what was wrong with England that it needed all this propaganda. I stopped at a small pub and ordered Courage's bitter beer. They were much relieved.

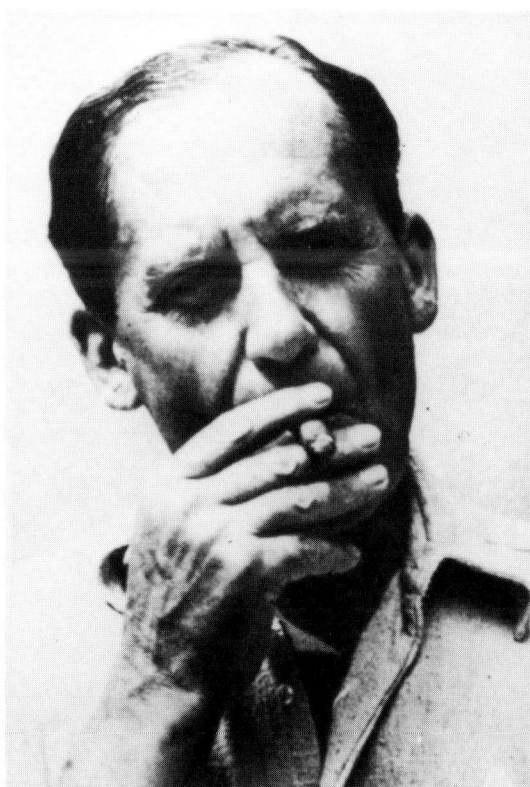

42. Walter Gropius at the time he came to England. He lived at Lawn Road Flats from 1934 until 1937

Not long after their arrival, we heard that two or three more Village Colleges were to be built. It was therefore arranged that Gropius and Henry Morris should meet in the Lawn Road Flats. It was a fruitful meeting. Although Gropius's English was only just developing, it was remarkable how quickly they understood each other.

They met again as Henry's guests in his elegant rooms in Trinity Street, Cambridge, which were somewhat seventeenth-century in character. Henry described that meeting in a letter to a friend: 'I had Gropius, the German architect, staying with me a few weeks ago (with a wife, exceptionally beautiful and equally intelligent – a marvellous combination), and his conversation and many months of study of modern architectural techniques confirm me in the necessity of doing all contemporary buildings without regard to traditional style.'

These meetings led directly to Walter Gropius and Max Fry designing Impington Village College, the episode I have described in detail in my earlier chapter on Henry Morris.

When we invited Gropius to England, I had also had high hopes for two building schemes in Manchester and Birmingham.

43. First birthday party for Lawn Road Flats: a tenant on the roof with Breuer and Ise and Walter Gropius

A.P.Simon, a member of the DIA, had a house in Didsbury, overlooking a small river to the south with sufficient land. It would make a good site for a small block of flats. He was enthusiastic and would join us and put in the land as his share.

The site in Birmingham was on land owned by Professor Philip Sargent Florence where he had a large house with plenty of land including a lake. Both provided good opportunities, sketch plans were produced, but both schemes fell through for somewhat similar reasons. Old covenants made development difficult if not impossible, and in Birmingham there was also much local opposition.

Windsor was a very different matter. The site available was on St Leonard's Hill overlooking Windsor Great Park. Windsor Castle could be seen in the distance. Here was an opportunity to preserve acres of gardens and lawns with a magnificent view over several counties and within easy reach of the city of London. The plan was to preserve by development. The choice was either to build a series of charming architectural houses or find some other way. In the *Architectural Review* of May 1935, there is a very good description of the whole idea. The title was 'Cry Stop to Havoc or Preservation by Development'.

If we built a series of houses, however well laid out, it would mean cutting down many very fine trees, and destroying lawns and gardens. An alternative was to do what was done by the aristocracy when they built the great country houses of England. There would be a fine mansion, well-laid-out gardens and a park.

Our plan was to design a mansion so as to provide a high degree of civilized living for the equivalent number of people who would occupy houses built on the estate. Domestic service would be included in the rent. There would be a play place for children, and to satisfy enthusiastic gardeners a plot could be arranged. The park, the fine trees, the existing lawns and gardens would be preserved.

An option was bought, a company formed. There was a meeting in London where a model of the buildings designed by Gropius and Fry was shown. Money was coming in; Hugh Weeks, the Director of Statistics and Programmes with whom I was to work later on in wartime, was then employed by Cadbury's, and he persuaded Lawrence Cadbury to subscribe a handsome sum. We had made it a condition that all money would be returned if the full amount was not subscribed.

I then fell ill and had to have an operation, and there was no one to keep up the momentum, so although the money was coming in at a rate that would almost meet our deadline, we failed. I wonder now whether my illness could have been psychosomatic and that I was afraid the venture was too big for me.

It *was* a great scheme and would have provided a fine example.

But, as it unfortunately turned out, Henry Morris was the only one in England with sufficient imagination to use Gropius for a public building, and since there were no other significant projects for him here, except a couple of houses, Gropius had to accept the chair he had been offered at Harvard. He left in 1937. Max Fry, with the help of Jack Howe, supervised the construction of Impington, occasionally consulting Walter in America. The building was completed just in time to be blacked out for the war.

When Gropius had first arrived in England the Isokon Furniture Company had only recently been formed, and Gropius agreed to become Controller of Design for the infant company; his help and advice were invaluable. He immediately advised that we should invite Marcel Breuer to design the furniture. (What happened then is described later, in my chapter about Breuer.)

Working with Gropius on the furniture and on the abortive building schemes, I found him easy and trusting. There was none of the difficulty I had had with Wells Coates, and was indeed later to experience with Breuer.

It is difficult to pinpoint any special influence Gropius had on me. In my relationship with Henry Morris there was a high proportion of emotion as well as intellect. So too with Walter. It was the total scene that he was concerned with: architecture and industrial design were a part of a whole, and so was music; the whole also included the attitude to people and to affairs generally. He made, as it were, a synthesis of life's work. He was concerned with all the various activities of the whole person in a community.

For a full life it was impossible to divide activities into separate compartments. A job should not only be concerned with making a living but should be worth doing in itself.

In a different way, much later on, he made this point when, after receiving the Albert Medal, he spoke at the RSA Dinner in his honour on 9 November 1961. Referring to the Bauhaus, he said:

> You may wonder how these ideas can make their way today in a period which, far from being dominated by the artist, does not even reflect the desires of the manufacturers, nor for that matter, the public demand, but is characterized by the power of the sales propagandist, of what your Mr Toynbee calls the 'Tempters', or what in the States are called 'the Madison Avenue Boys'. Under their regime it seems completely futile to inject quality into buildings and goods which are created only for their short entertainment value before they are discarded or exchanged for another set of equally ephemeral items.

After referring to the importance of education he wound up by saying:

> For me there isn't much more time to carry on the work, but I hope that England, the most mature country of the Western world, the most conscious of the power of education, will produce men who will eventually blaze a trail out of the commercial jungle in which we are entangled, for it seems to be unimaginable that human nature should not eventually rebel against the conspiracy to replace the 'tree of life' with a sales spiral.

The last serious conversation I had with him was when Molly and I were invited by his partners in Cambridge, Massachusetts, to be at his eighty-fifth birthday. The day after the celebration, we had lunch together at his house in Lincoln, Massachusetts.

We saw him once more, in January 1968 on our way to Australia. He had just returned from a trip to Mexico and South America on some job. He looked frail; he hoped we could stay a while and have a talk, but our timetable made that impossible. I should have cancelled our programme and stayed a while and seen him again in Lincoln.

In April 1933, when the activities of the Hitler gangsters were increasing, Gropius had already been arrested by the Criminal Police, and later three brown-shirted Nazi gangsters entered his office and ordered him not to go again to an exhibition where he had designed a stand for the German non-ferrous industry. Gropius was clearly aware of the danger he was in.

'Cremate me,' he wrote,

> but ask not for the ashes. The piety for cinders is a halfway thing. Out with it. Wear no signs of mourning. It would be beautiful if all my friends of the present and of the past would get together in a little while for a fiesta – à la Bauhaus – drinking, laughing, loving. Then I shall surely join in, more than in life. It is more fruitful than the graveyard oratory. Love is the essence of everything.

When Walter died in 1969 at the age of eighty-six, Ise had the courage to have a party à la Bauhaus; it was on Friday 8 May 1970, and she called it a Metallic Festival and, as found before at the 'Metallic Festival' held at the Bauhaus in Dessau in 1929, the only way into the party was down a chute.

The significance of Gropius and the Bauhaus remains, but is seldom understood.

There were three principles.

The first was to find ways to break down any preconceived ideas the students might have and set them free to develop their own personalities to the fullest extent and give vitality to their thinking.

The second was that students must be professional in hand work, finding new ways to achieve perfection.

The third, by which I was particularly impressed, was based on what Gropius wrote in 1923. He was calling for a balance between art and science, in terms not unlike those of Henry Morris, who wrote that the only pursuit in life was science and art and to bathe in them was our constant medium. According to Gropius:

> True creative work can only be done by the man whose knowledge and mastery of the physical laws of statics, dynamics, optics and acoustics equip him to give life and shape to his inner vision.

> In a work of art, the laws of the physical world, the intellectual world

and the world of the spirit must be expressed simultaneously

A clear call for a marriage between art and science. Some of these ideas were foreshadowed by Peter Kropotkin in 1899. He wrote in *Field, Factories and Workshops* that, while specialization is necessary, it must follow general education and must include science and handcraft. Otherwise society will continue to be divided into brain workers and manual workers.

Gropius's third principle calls for some degree of science in the curriculum, but in practice there was little opportunity for that to be introduced. The Bauhaus lived for only a little over ten years before being destroyed by the Nazis. Even during those years the Bauhaus teachers were spending too much time fighting for their existence – as educationalists are having to do today.

When referring to a marriage between art and science some artists and designers complain that this is as impossible as trying to mix water and oil. But the great Swiss psychologist Jean Piaget has shown how children almost from birth are trying to find out how things happen. They are not so much playing; they are doing and thinking – learning how to think. They make experiments and, having discovered how something happens, they will repeat it, to see if it does it again. Later they learn measurement – how far will a ball roll? Of course this applies whether the child later becomes an artist or scientist.

'I want the students,' Gropius once said, 'independently to create true, genuine forms of the technical, economic and social conditions – unbiased, original.'

He also said: 'There are many branches on the Bauhaus tree and on them sit many different kinds of birds.'

The Gropius Architecture Exhibition, and how it came to Britain

In 1970, when Ise told me that a Gropius exhibition was travelling round the world but no request for it had come from Britain, I had a word with Peter Shepheard, one of Molly's bird-watching friends, then the president of the Royal Institute of British Architects. The RIBA were interested in showing the exhibition, but when they heard from the Bauhaus Archive it was found to be too large for their exhibition space. The Arts Council was then offered it; it took them five months to say 'No'.

This apparent official indifference to an exhibition which, as I realized from my own experience of lecturing, was likely to arouse widespread public interest in Britain, seemed very odd. Corin Hughes-Stanton, then

44. With Walter Gropius at Harvard, during Gropius's eighty-fifth birthday celebrations

editor of *Design* magazine, took the story up and put a paragraph in the issue for April 1972. This was followed with a letter to *The Times*, quoting from *Design*, signed by many influential people and published on 17 June 1972. There was then an immediate response, with several cities asking for the exhibition. The calls came from Cardiff, Belfast, Dublin, Glasgow, Bristol, Edinburgh, Brighton and Manchester. A request to show the exhibition also came from Impington, the Village College which Gropius had designed.

The letter in *The Times* was also spotted by Gontran Goulden, director general of the Building Centre in London, and he wrote to the Bauhaus Archive offering to sponsor the exhibition in Britain, including the administration and cash to start it off. It was an imaginative offer.

Meanwhile Ken Baynes, who had had his own plans to put on the exhibition in Wales and Scotland, generously came in with all his own connections and experience. There was now a good team, Gudrun Simmonds at the Bauhaus Archive in Darmstadt, the Building Centre in London and Ken Baynes.

We then remembered the effectiveness of the Nehru Memorial Exhibition held in the Festival Hall, which had been designed by Charles and Ray Eames. They brought life and shape to it by showing pictures of the young Nehru and his family set against illustrations of important events at the various stages of his life. We used the same approach for the Gropius exhibition, putting his life and work into the context of his time.

Ise was delighted with our plans and came over for the opening at the Building Centre in London on 2 February 1974. She made a fine opening speech and gave a lecture, answering many questions. She was magnificent. She also came to the Manchester exhibition with her sister.

David Elliott, who later became director of the Museum of Modern Art in Oxford, produced a brief, lucid account of the life and work of Walter Gropius in England, and the Design and Industries Association produced a time chart of important events from 1901 to Gropius's death in 1969. The Glasgow showing was largely sponsored by the Goethe Institute, and was held in the Art Gallery and Museum, where Max Fry made a splendid opening speech, high up on the grand staircase looking down on the audience, which included stuffed prehistoric animals. The exhibition in Impington Village College was for me the most moving; it just fitted into the great corridor.

11
Marcel Breuer

I met Marcel Breuer when he came to Britain for the first time, in 1935. F.R.S. Yorke had invited him to be a partner in his architectural practice.

His arrival one morning in the Lawn Road Flats caused anger, confusion and delight. Carola Giedion and Sybil Moholy were sharing a flat for a while, and Sybil had received a book from Breuer which, when opened, was found to be *Mein Kampf*. It was worse than a poor joke, she and Carola were furious and threw it away with the rubbish.

Breuer arrived soon after, apparently happy at being away from Nazi Germany, only to find two furious dames attacking him with no mercy. When he could get a word in he explained that, in order to get some of his money through the German Customs, he thought it would be a bright idea to interleave their leader's great book with bank-notes. They would surely not examine it with any great care.

There was immediate pandemonium, all rushed down, hoping the rubbish had not yet been taken away. When they found the book, all was forgiven.

As I got to know him, I found Breuer full of fun and mischief, but his English was very poor.

Soon after his arrival there was a meeting of the Half Hundred dining club; he came as my guest. It was Raymond Postgate's turn to be in charge of the menu. He explained that there was no special merit in the soup except that it remained blue all the way through. We all laughed, including Breuer. Someone got up, left the table, and came back saying, 'Yes, it does'. There was more laughter.

That night at about midnight Breuer rang up in great distress – was I all right? I then realized what had happened: he had not understood a word and he found the blue alarming.

Gropius was then Controller of Design for the infant Isokon: a company set up by Molly, Wells Coates and myself to promote buildings and furniture of strictly modern functional design. Gropius said we should ask Breuer to be the designer for Isokon. I found Breuer difficult to come to terms with. He found me difficult too and in December 1935 wrote to Gropius about the problems of coming to terms with me. But once he was with us he proved easy to work with. He started in January 1936. The terms agreed were a royalty of 5 per cent of trade price of the furniture (or the price paid by the customers) and a retainer of two or three hundred pounds a year.

Gropius suggested that, with my connections with Venesta, Breuer should design a long chair in plywood. Molly and I had already seen his previous design for a long chair in Duralumin in Switzerland. Harry Mansell, a wonderful craftsman who was not afraid of new ideas, had already joined us at Isokon, and the three of them made a splendid team. The result was a remarkable piece of construction, quite different from the Swiss chair.

The opening sentence of the US patent makes the point: 'The essence of this invention is the construction of a chair with a resilient plywood or similar sheet material, which itself forms part of and completes a closed chair frame. There is no complete frame until the seat is applied, and by making the chair in this way, striking resilience and comfort are obtained.' It becomes a structure in itself.

Clive Entwistle, when describing the Isokon Long Chair, wrote that it had an economy of line and form comparable with that of a leopard or an orchid.

There was great excitement in the early days when we received an order for a dozen of these chairs from Dolphin Square. This building had an indoor swimming pool, and the Isokon Long Chairs were placed around the pool. The floor was tiled and the tiles were warmed, and our first chair was made using Scotch glue, easy and flexible in use but soluble when warm and damp. It was not long before our precious chairs became, as John Gloag described them, 'an embarrassing collection of veneer'.

The lesson was learnt fast, and we then used a new ICI product that was not soluble under Dolphin Square conditions. It was not long before Bassett-Lowke had two or three Long Chairs installed in a municipal

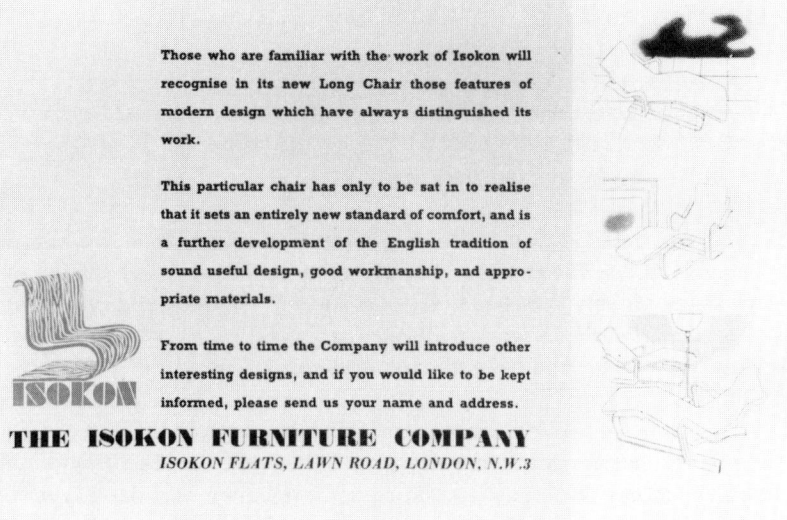

45. Moholy-Nagy's original advertisement for the Isokon Long Chair

46. The Long Chair in bent plywood, designed by Marcel Breuer for Isokon in 1936 and still in production

bath-house in similar conditions to Dolphin Square, and they stood up well.

All of Breuer's pieces of Isokon furniture have a unique simplicity. The table has an added quality. It stands firm on an uneven floor; both firmness and flexibility are provided by the curved sides.

Breuer's first design for a stacking chair came too soon. Had we had at that time the powerful adhesives we have now, the chair could have been made almost in one operation. When bent or shaped laminations are put under closing pressure so that the laminations are pressed together, the strength can be maintained, but once the pressure is in reverse, the adhesives have to be powerful otherwise they will separate. This is the problem we encountered.

After the war, Arne Jacobsen in Denmark was able to take advantage of the new powerful adhesives and design a seat and back formed out of one piece of plywood. He was also able to make a slightly double curve

47. The Isokon Dining Table designed by Breuer in 1936. Slightly curving sides enable it to stand firm even on an uneven floor

48. Molly's consulting-room in Upper Harley Street, planned by Christopher Nicholson. Note the Isokon tables and John Piper picture on the wall

 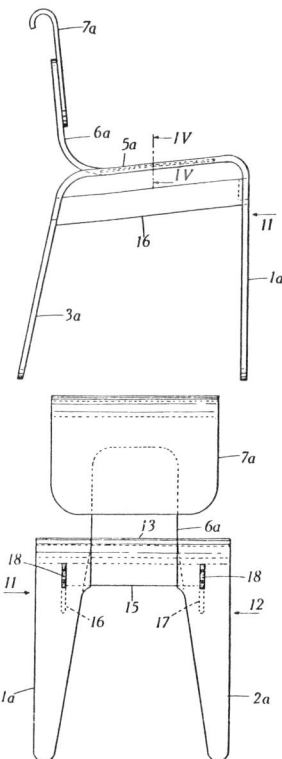

to give extra firmness and flexibility at the same time. But the difference was that his chair was in two parts, the seat and back forming one part and the set of legs the other, whereas the Breuer chair was one complete whole.

Production of Breuer's Isokon furniture began in 1937, and by 1939 we were making and selling up to nine Long Chairs each week.

Both Gropius and Breuer left for the USA in 1937, as previously explained; fortunately for the continuity of the Isokon design programme, the Viennese architect Egon Riss had also escaped from Nazi Austria to the Lawn Road Flats. In return for somewhat elementary accommodation, he stoked the boilers and did other odd jobs. As the wartime dangers worsened, he used sandbags to build what he called the Isokon Line – protecting the windows and the open air restaurant.

Riss also produced designs for furniture, which had great wit and charm. When Allen Lane saw the 'Donkey' he was greatly impressed and offered some 100,000 advertising leaflets to go into his Penguin books, free of charge. The 'Donkey' was then renamed the 'Isokon Penguin Donkey':

49. (*Left*) Prototype Isokon Dining Chair, designed by Marcel Breuer, first produced in 1937. (*Right*) Working drawings for the production version, which required reinforcements. An upholstered version was also produced

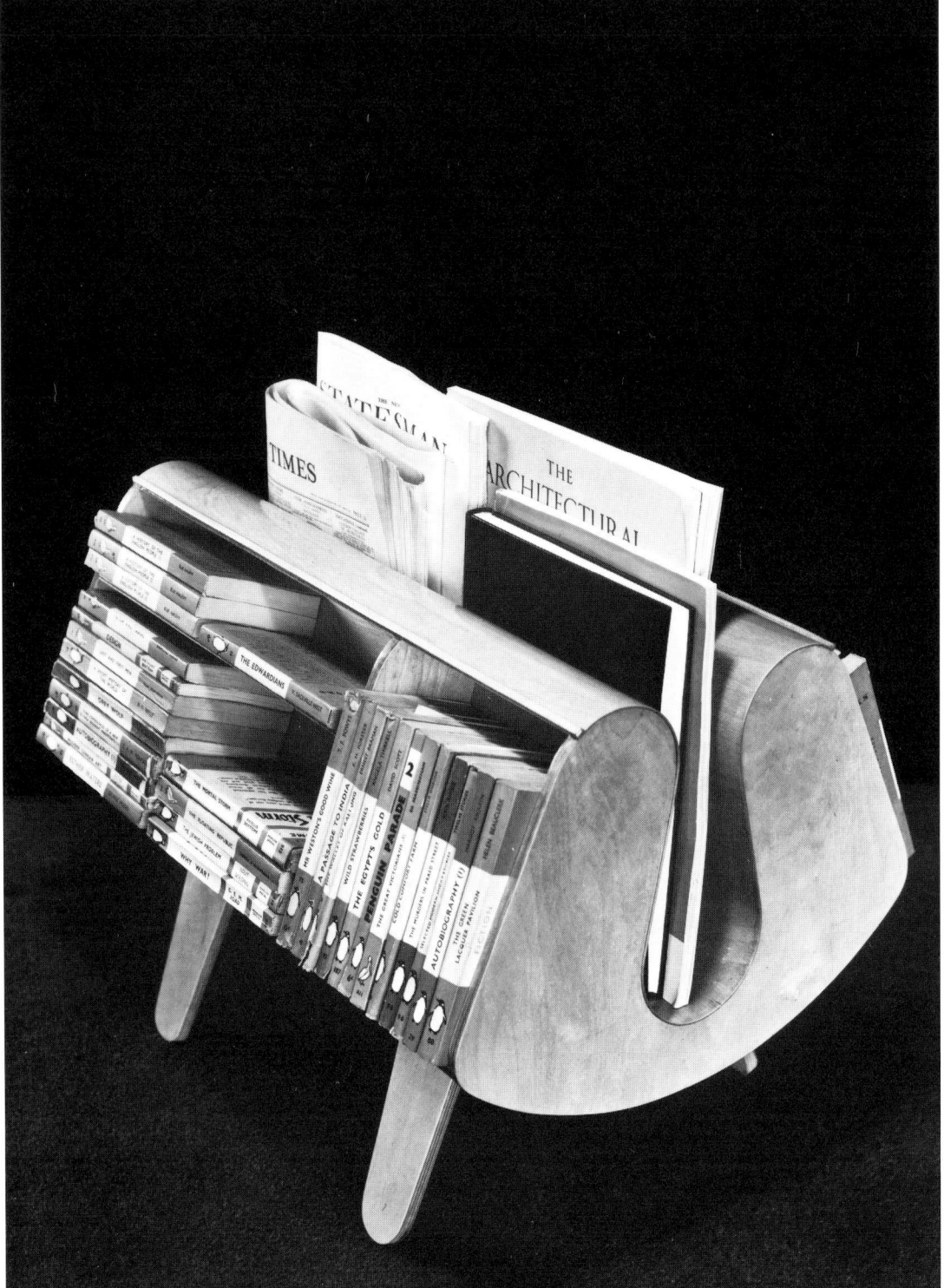

'Donkey' because it had four legs and two panniers – its body was hollow to provide space for papers. Production was started, but the war came too soon. Allen had to stop the leaflets; we had to stop production. The hundred which had been made were snapped up at once. After the war, Ernest Race redesigned the 'Donkey' and thousands were sold through Penguin Books.

Egon also designed a 'Bottleship' and 'Pocket Bottleship', both witty and efficient. The prototypes were made by Pfiefer in Camden Town; only the 'Pocket Bottleship' and its companion the 'Gull' survive.

50. The Isokon Penguin Donkey Mark I (*opposite*)
51. The Isokon Pocket Bottleship (*above left*), both designed by Egon Riss in 1939
52. Ernest Race's Mark 2 Bottleship (*above*), the postwar KD design
53. Prototype Square Table designed by Walter Gropius in 1936, but not produced

Selling the Isokon Penguin Donkey had its amusing side. One day a friendly voice came over the telephone saying his son had received one. I asked if he liked it; oh yes, but his son was three years old. Another time a policeman rang saying that a highly indignant man had received a carton containing an unasked-for Donkey, and complained of improper selling methods. When I told the policeman that a few people would play tricks and send the reply postcard addressed to someone to pull their leg, the conversation ended in chuckles.

In the Donkey leaflet for Penguin Books we showed the Long Chair and the Donkey side by side. As a result we had a few sales of the Long Chair as well; but the chair did not sell well through the retail shops. Heals would not sell it with the name Isokon, so Breuer designed a different Long Chair for sale through Heals. It had none of the original's remarkable character or resilience. John Gloag introduced me to Geoffrey Dunn,

who immediately understood the significance of the Isokon Long Chair and showed it in his very fine shop, Dunns of Bromley – but still it did not sell.

Looking back now, I am puzzled that we made hardly any of the Breuer Short Chairs, and in the USA I know of just the one Long Chair: in the Gropius house.

Isokon furniture was restarted around 1970. Sam Green from Remploy had known about Isokon from way back, so production was made easy. The Long Chair was made near London, and the redesigned Isokon Penguin Donkey was made in large quantities in the West Country. The Donkey was partly KD, very easy to assemble and packed in cartons complete with screwdriver.

Herbert Spencer designed a range of stationery, and Remploy dispatched the Donkeys. When I told Nikolaus Pevsner of the return of Isokon, he was delighted and wrote a charming welcoming message for us to use on our leaflets. The original Long Chair folders had been designed by Moholy-Nagy.

The furniture business was run very efficiently by Christine Webber, my secretary, from one of the Lawn Road flats, which was used for the

54. Geoffrey Dunn, proprietor of Dunn's of Bromley and one of the first stockists of the Isokon Long Chair, admiring my Dursley-Pedersen bicycle

55. Egon Riss building the 'Isokon Line' at Lawn Road Flats in wartime

56. 'Breuer and Moholy-Nagy go to America': cartoon by Gordon Cullen, 1937

57. Harry Mansell and myself delivering a Long Chair by canoe to a customer near Oxford, c. 1940

58. Advertisement for the Isokon Penguin Donkey Mark 2, the version designed after the war by Ernest Race. The man in the Long Chair is, needless to say, myself

Here it is

This obliging creature holds up to ninety Penguin books in two panniers, carries a number of magazines between these panniers and provides a convenient chairside table for your tray of hors d'oeuvres, coffee cups, glass, ashtray, knitting or anything else you want to keep beside you. Beautifully designed by the late Ernest Race, the Penguin Donkey gives you a talking-point centrepiece for your room. The Donkey is eggshell-finished in white acid catalyst enamel – a surface unaffected by hot cups or spilt drinks, a surface that wipes clean with a touch. The horizontal shelves are horizontal because Penguins *should* lie flat. They keep better that way and you can read every title from your chair. The upright spaces? They take maps, hardbacks, Peregrines, what-have-you.
And for you, we've saved the pleasure of final assembly. It involves the turning of eight screws (we provide the screw driver) which gives you five minutes of delicious do-it-yourself satisfaction, followed by years of faithful service.

Isokon Penguin Donkey Mark 2

DONKEY DATA
The body is made of best quality plywood with an oyster white acid catalyst enamel finish. The legs are natural West African mahogany and the assembly screws are sleeved, metal to metal, for easy and permanent fixing.
Overall height 15½"
Overall length 20½"
Overall width 15½"

Designed by Ernest Race FSIA for the Isokon Furniture Company. Accepted by the Council of Industrial Design for inclusion in the Design Register.

Patent application No 26407'63
Design application No 911722

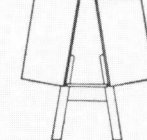
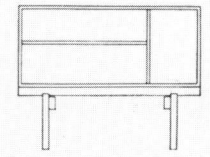

management of the building. The business was profitable and going well when Christine said that she and her husband wanted to start a small business and asked if they could run Isokon for us. For a time it worked well, but as they began to develop furniture items of a very different character the arrangement was not so satisfactory and eventually we had to part company.

We saw Breuer once or twice after he left us for America, and stayed with him and his wife, Connie, in their home in Connecticut. His houses were a delight – direct, original and practical. He was one of the most original architects I have known.

Breuer's short partnership with Gropius broke up early, and then we saw less and less of him. Once in New York I asked him what were the basic ideas that made the Bauhaus important. His reply was strange. 'Nothing', he said, 'but the coincidence of a group of people happening to come together at the same time.'

Breuer wrote:

> The eye is a powerful informer, it forms an aesthetic judgement at a glance and, while buildings should be useful, well constructed and in harmony with our human–social world, the first impact, the eye impact, is perhaps a preconditioning of our sympathies.

That is very much Breuer. And again:

> In the agony of search for a precise formulation, once, quite a few years ago, I wrote my first and only poem (of a sort):
>
>> Colours which you can hear with ears;
>> Sounds to see with eyes;
>> The void you touch with your elbows;
>> The taste of space on your tongue;
>> The fragrance of dimensions;
>> The juice of a stone.

At about the same time he wrote:

> It has been argued that if a chair is beautiful it is also comfortable. This is just as questionable as to say: if it is comfortable it is also beautiful. No beauty can make us forget that man needs something to sit on, and that he needs to sit comfortably, and that this something is the instrument which we call a chair.

Marcel Breuer died at the age of seventy-nine on 1 July 1981 in the USA.

12
Moholy-Nagy

Laszlo Moholy-Nagy was born in a small town in Hungary in July 1895, and his early life was hard. He went through the war of 1914–18 in Galicia on the Russian front, surviving the collapse of the Austro-Hungarian Empire and then the Hungarian Revolution.

Already by 1917, when he was twenty-three, he was interested in light; he wrote in a poem, 'Learn to know the light design of your life', and again, 'space, time, material and they are one with light'. (This is somewhat similar to the poem written by Breuer quoted in the previous chapter.)

Moholy took a law degree in Budapest and then, a penniless exile in Vienna, he took a slow train to Berlin, stopping at small towns where he did odd jobs to earn a few pfennigs.

By the time he got to Berlin he was so exhausted that he collapsed, and fortunately he was found by a couple of Quakers, who helped him. He worked at any job until he found his real vocation: photography and advertising.

Moholy was apparently somewhat scatterbrained. He was fortunate to meet Lucia, his first wife; she gave him the mental discipline that lasted for the rest of his life. Sibyl Moholy, his second wife, has written about this in *Experiment in Totality*.

When Walter Gropius heard of Moholy and his work they met, and in 1923 he was offered the post of master in charge of the Advanced Foundation Course of the Metal Shop at the Bauhaus. That gave Moholy his great opportunity to develop himself to the full. He was still under thirty. Soon he became a great and inspired teacher and remained one for the rest of his life.

Richard Filipowski, a student of his in Chicago, wrote in 1944: 'Moholy never criticized the work of a student in terms of good or bad . . . nothing was all bad; each idea contained a spark of quality' (*Experiment in Totality*).

In 1928 Walter Gropius resigned from the Bauhaus in the face of increasing administrative difficulties and political pressures, and so Moholy, Breuer, Kandinsky, Bayer and others did too. Moholy wrote a powerful letter of resignation deploring the pressure for greater emphasis on vocational training that left no time for the whole man, and wound up with: 'The question arises whether the existence of a creative group is only possible on the basis of opposition to the status quo.'

He went back to Berlin and soon found plenty of work, including the fascinating stage-sets for the *Tales of Hoffmann*, *Madam Butterfly* and *The Merchant of Berlin*, but the Nazi power was becoming too strong; he would have preferred to face and fight, but that was not possible, so he went to Holland. There he studied recent developments in colour photography, believing that the new technology would have its full expression in the development of abstract composition.

He then decided to go to England – largely, he said, for two reasons: the English people's love of free speech (he said he was strongly influenced by Voltaire's *Lettres Philosophiques sur les Anglais*) and their amateurism.

I first met Moholy in May 1935 when he came to the Lawn Road Flats. He had a magnificent, infectious grin. His work was already known in London, especially amongst young designers and architects, and advertising agencies. John Gloag had visited him in Berlin.

I had Moholy do a full-page advertisement for Venesta in the *Architectural Review*. The brief was simple: to indicate that Venesta plywood was both rigid and flexible, and to avoid any emphasis on the technical quality or the company's policy. He worked fast; at first it seemed to me that he was too facile, but I soon realized that his speed was due to his speed of understanding and execution at the same time – analysis and synthesis almost in one operation. The result was a picture of a stylized tree of thick plywood, wrapped round with a sheet of very thin plywood by way of contrast. The tree was brown, standing in front of a green smudge occupying most of the background – typical of Moholy. The whole effect was good, and the advertisement appeared in the *Review* of February 1936. It certainly had quite a strong impact on younger architects.

59. Moholy-Nagy in the mid-1930s

Within the firm many thought the advertisement was a waste of money, as it did not describe the technical merits of Venesta plywood; but the chairman, Henry Rutherford, had tolerance and gave me plenty of rope. His son, Harry Rutherford, told me later that his father had often said that I had many good and imaginative ideas, some of which might have made good profit, others of which might have driven them into bankruptcy; the trouble was how to choose.

When Breuer's Isokon Long Chair was ready to be launched, Moholy designed a folder showing two people sitting in the chairs facing each other, with a light and a table between them. The scene was staged in our flat. The leaflet included a small drawing of a figure floating in a bath, suggesting that reclining in a Breuer Long Chair was rather similar. This I called the Archimedes principle of comfort. By supporting the body over a wide area, the pressure per square inch would be small and so greater comfort would be achieved.

There was another principle. Dr Akerblom, a Swedish doctor specializing in seating problems, suggested that comfort could be obtained by sitting upright and concentrating all the body weight on the ischial tuberosities, i.e. towards the bones at the base of the pelvis. I believed that his theory could be developed.

When we were trying to launch Gropius's and Fry's 'Windsor' scheme, I should have asked Moholy to design the folder, but instead I asked my brother, Fleetwood, and his firm to do the job. They had a high reputation for sound marketing and advertising and produced a conventional job – but it had no charisma. Had Moholy done the job, it would have had a far more powerful influence and might have tipped the balance;

as it was, we were not far off from success. Anyway, such a folder by Moholy would have provided a fine record of a good idea that failed.

By 1936 Moholy, with the help of George Kepes, had achieved a great deal of work in London, which included working for Simpsons in the Strand, and producing a film on the sex life of the lobster. He was also asked to film the Olympic Games in Berlin.

He went to Berlin and, entering the stadium, was enthusiastically welcomed by a former Bauhaus man in the uniform of an SS officer. This man whispered to Moholy, suggesting to him that by joining the Nazis he might have some influence and be ready when the chance came. But from what he was told and the way it was said Moholy was convinced that the man had sold out to the Nazis. Moholy saw little of the sports and telephoned London that he would not do the film and would have nothing further to do with Nazi Germany.

Moholy's first one-man exhibition in London was arranged by Peter Norton in the London Gallery in Cork Street.

Moholy had a wonderful way of using words as if in error or through not understanding the language – sometimes, I suspect, on purpose. On one occasion John Betjeman had taken him to a party. As Moholy left he said to the hostess in his strange pronunciation; 'Thank you for your hostilities.' She was a little taken aback, and when Moholy told John Betjeman what had happened, Betjeman said: 'Oh don't worry – she is hostile to everyone.'

I introduced Moholy to Henry Morris and took him on one of Henry's walks. Henry and Gropius had understood one another immediately, but Henry could not make head or tail of Moholy. He understood and admired Moholy's ideas on colour, and I believe he used his ideas in one or other of the Village Colleges, but as a person he found him a puzzle.

Henry always insisted on the importance of hanging original paintings on the walls of schools in preference to prints, but Moholy thought otherwise and once wrote: 'I could not find any argument against the wide distribution of works of art, even if turned out by mass production' (L. Moholy-Nagy, *Abstract of an Artist*, 1944).

Henry Moore made, I believe, about seven from one cast of his small maquettes. Would I mind if he made 700 or even 700,000? Would it make any difference to the pleasure I get from looking at mine? I wonder.

In July 1937 Moholy received a cable from America with offers of financial support from Marshall Field, Paepeke of the Container Corporation, Montgomery Ward and other rich and well-known men of commerce.

Sibyl was doubtful, misunderstood the name of one of the sponsors, and advised Moholy to have nothing to do with the army and field marshals. Moholy decided to go to America to meet them anyway.

I took Moholy to Waterloo Station to catch the boat train to Southampton for the SS *Manhattan*. Meetings had been fixed immediately on his arrival in the USA, and Moholy had packed essential material to demonstrate his ideas in a case with special locks which was to go as hand luggage.

About ten minutes before the train was due to leave, he searched for the keys but found he had left them in his house in Golders Green!

After a quick talk with the railway inspector I decided that there was a good chance that I could get the keys to Moholy at the ship, provided all went well. Kepes, Moholy's assistant, was to come with me to find the keys. We said goodbye to a very worried Moholy.

With Kepes I went back to Moholy's flat, found the keys, cancelled meetings at my office and telephoned the AA. I told them what I had to do, and described the car and my route. I would have to average nearly forty miles an hour and our Rover 12 was getting old. I asked Kepes to check our average speed every quarter of an hour, and as soon as we reached the average of forty miles an hour I began to slow down.

As we came to a long straight part of the Basingstoke by-pass, I saw in the distance an AA box and two of their scouts standing by. Then one went to the telephone box, came out, spotted us and told us we were a bit late – keep going, they told us, and as we approached Southampton we would see one of their scouts on a motor bike on the left-hand side of the road. His engine would be running. He saw us as soon as we saw him and started off with us following him.

He led us through a complicated route, travelling fast, and then drove straight through the dock gates which were opened for us by the police, who had been warned by the AA. We had ten or fifteen minutes to spare.

Moholy was overjoyed and embraced us delightedly. Kepes and I returned to London happy. We drove the car more gently on the way back.

Amongst our pictures by Moholy is a print of a nude. When I went up to open an exhibition of his works in Glasgow in 1978, I arrived with some of our own pictures which were to be included in the exhibition; but instead of the print of the nude that he had given us I had had it reproduced – a photograph of a photograph. Moholy would have approved, even perhaps preferring to have used the negative. Some time ago on seeing the photograph of the nude, a friend said; 'I didn't know you had a photograph of me.' Not long after, another friend on seeing it said much the same.

In the winter of 1944–5 when, as I explain later, I was sent to the USA for the Ministry of Fuel and Power, I had to go to Chicago, and Moholy took me to see his design school. The only time that we could meet to make the visit was one night after supper. The school at that time was over the old slaughterhouses, and to get in we had to go through mysterious caverns, take a lift, then walk through the kitchens of a night club, and so into the school. To the dismay of the staff in the kitchen Moholy tasted the delicious morsels being prepared as we walked through – but his captivating smile worked wonders!

Moholy ran the school on much the same lines as the Bauhaus in Dessau, devising ways to stretch the imagination of his students, and this was evident in the work we saw.

I saw his light machine in mobile glass and metal which was used for the abstract film *Light Play Black-White-Grey* of 1925–30. A ping-pong ball floated without visible support, though it was of course held up by a jet of air. Why not, he said, use this method for a chair?

Until I read Sibyl Moholy's *Experiment in Totality*, I did not appreciate the extreme difficulty Moholy had in trying to run a design school in the US. Within a year the sponsors, in whom he had such great confidence, proved broken reeds and financial support dried up. They had wanted vocational courses that would train industrial designers. But that would only produce mediocrity not creative designers.

After the first failure he started again, and then again. When the war came, short courses for GIs were called for. He provided them and this helped to pay for long-term students. He had a hard time of it – though he always recovered and tried again. But Moholy never found sponsors who really understood and accepted his ideas or gave him a framework in which to develop unmolested.

In November 1945 he collapsed and entered hospital – he had leukemia. He had to select the illustrations for his book *Vision in Motion* while in hospital and was desperate to get it finished. He was also struggling with his sculpture in moulded sheets of plexiglass, finding the cutting more and more difficult.

In January 1946 he was out of hospital and back at his old intensive work, believing he had made a full recovery. The institute at this point had to move again – this time to Dearborn Street; the building looked like a stone fortress.

In November an urgent call came for him to attend a meeting at the

Museum of Modern Art under the chairmanship of Joseph Hudnut, Dean of Harvard University. Moholy was just out of hospital. In spite of advice not to go, he went, and was stimulated by the meeting, afterwards going on to a party. He was in good form, but people noticed how ill he was. He returned home with a high temperature; again he dragged himself to another meeting, and this time went straight back to hospital.

Before he died on 24 November 1946, he called for crayons and went on drawing.

In December 1948 I was again in America, and called on Sibyl and purchased three pictures by Moholy; one of which is the crayon drawing Moholy completed just before he died.

WAR AND POSTWAR

13
Ministry of Information and Ministry of Supply

When the war started it was quite clear that my small Isokon furniture business would be unable to go on; the essential supplies of plywood parts for assembly would dry up, and anyway we only had a couple of men working and it would not be possible to get any war contracts, however small.

The flats had been going badly. As war rumours began, it was harder to get people to take long leases. I made the mistake of thinking that war might not come yet, and continued to insist on long leases; of course, later, when the danger of bombing became evident, a reinforced concrete building was attractive, and we began to do better again. Meanwhile we were getting empty flats and I would be needing a job.

My cousin Esmond had been pulled in to the Ministry of Information and suggested that I might do the same. They took me on in the press censorship department, first censoring illustrations for publication.

On joining the department, I saw a group of very important- and distinguished-looking men in earnest conversation. I joined them. Should members of the section wear uniform? If they did they would have to travel first class, go into the bar parlour rather than the public bar and all that would be expensive – on the other hand, shouldn't we maintain the dignity of the services? At first I thought it a bit of joke, but they were serious. When we were asked in turn what we thought I said, 'Uniform.' On being asked what had been my rank, I said midshipman. Clearly I had got off on the wrong foot.

One time going home after night duty I was pedalling my bike – a very fine specimen of a Dursley-Pedersen with its hammock saddle and spindly frame. These machines were very light and had an early form of three-speed gear. They were produced during the first part of the century but went out around 1912. As I was pedalling up from the City towards the Angel – quite a stiff climb – I began to realize that there was a motor car following me, very slowly. Eventually it passed, and stopped in front of me. Out jumped two young policemen who asked for my papers, very politely. They soon apologized, saying that they thought I must be a foreigner, riding such a strange bicycle and wearing such strange clothes. I had on a fairly new suit cut in much the same style as a simplified Norfolk jacket.

We had some quite interesting stories to be censored. There was the one about a man who had sailed back to France in his large yacht – just at the time that the Germans had occupied Paris. He had remembered that he had left some confidential papers in his office and they might be useful for the Germans. So he took his Austin Seven on board and landed safely at Le Havre; he drove his little car to Paris, found his papers and drove back safely, getting back to England without difficulty. He then got quite a shock when he realized that his car had a GB plate on the back. I never heard why this story was censored; I often wonder if there was any truth in it.

The work was exciting when we heard important news – uncensored – especially, for me, the Battle of the River Plate between the *Graf Spee* and our more lightly-armed cruisers.

Going home at night could be quite exciting too. Once I got on my bike intending to ride down Gower Street, but we were directed by way of Russell Square. There was a smell of cordite and a few clouds of smoke, and I could feel the scrunch of rubble and broken glass under my wheels; again I was diverted, along Upper Woburn Place to cross Euston Road. There the traffic light went red; and although there was the sound of a few bombs not far away, I stopped to wait for the light to change. How strangely orderly we could be.

One Saturday afternoon I went to Cambridge to see Henry Morris. Returning to London on Sunday we were running on time until quite near Liverpool Street Station, where we could see large clouds of black smoke, lit up by flames. As we came into the station, not more than ten or fifteen minutes late, there was more smoke and noise and a sound not unlike a machine-gun. Yet few of us on the train took to our heels. Most of us walked, gave up our tickets – *then* we ran. At Moorgate it seemed that the station was on fire, but I walked in and bought my ticket as usual. The train came in as usual too, and I had supper in the Isobar, as usual.

But the work itself was routine and negative, and one day when Hugh Weeks was having dinner in the Isobar I told him what I was doing and how I wished I could find a more constructive job.

I had known Hugh when he was in Birmingham working with Cadbury's. It was Philip Sargent Florence who introduced me at the time we were trying to get the great Windsor scheme going. Hugh was impressed with the idea and had, as I mentioned earlier, persuaded Lawrence Cadbury to put up some money for the scheme. After that I saw Hugh occasionally, sometimes at Design and Industries Association meetings, and he rather liked the Isokon furniture.

He told me he was setting up a statistics section in the Ministry of Supply.

His job was to provide the Minister with a running commentary on how production of war materials was meeting War Office demands. It sounded highly complicated to me, but not apparently to Hugh. He was building up a team of those who could at least understand something about what constituted munitions; they should be able to cope with figures and to explain what the figures were about. It sounded fine, and really constructive.

When Hugh suggested that I should apply to join his outfit I was delighted. Though I was by no means a statistician I insisted on the proper use of statistics when I was at Venesta, and I expect that Hugh assumed that I was better at figures than I was. Some years after the war we got to know Hugh's deputy, Kenneth Usherwood, who became chairman of the Prudential (we see him and Mary, his wife, frequently now, as they have a cottage in Walberswick). Both Hugh and Kenneth have incredibly fast brains and the facility for making, with just a few figures, a complex situation simpler – very necessary for a busy minister. Kenneth teased me, and once said that the reason why I kept the job was that if I could understand the figures, then the Minister might.

Each week we had to produce a statistical report for the Minister. Every effort was made to reduce complexity; this was sometimes difficult, and continually raised the question of the multitude of necessary qualifications, and how to reduce or cut without loss of meaning. It would be a late session, and sometimes a few members of the department would come to the Isobar, and maybe stay the night if the bombing was troublesome.

The team grew, and included some who were already well established, such as David Glass and, of course, Gilbert Walker, who was soon to become a professor at Birmingham. Then there was that delightful, strange man, John Mandeville, with whom some years after the war our second son, Jeremy, gained experience in data processing and computing before setting up his own business.

The evenings at the Isobar had some lasting results. John Mandeville took a flat and also found a wife. I rather think something of the sort happened for Kenneth Usherwood, though he was not a resident.

Life could still be very peaceful at times. Sometimes on a Sunday I would take a train and then walk to Perry Green and have lunch with Irina and Henry Moore. I might take a bottle of wine or something to contribute. In the garden there was a small pile of hay; after lunch I would sleep on one side and Henry on the other. Sometimes Jacquetta Hawkes would come with me, and I also remember Polly Hill came with her bicycle.

I wanted to send a Henry Moore drawing to Walter Gropius in America:

but how to get it there? The problem seemed insoluble until early in December 1941, a few days after Pearl Harbor, Hugh Weeks came into my office one morning and said that if I could get the picture to him that evening, he might be able to find a way of getting it to Walter.

But the picture I wanted to send was in Henry's studio near Much Hadham. By a stroke of luck he was coming up to London that morning and would bring it with him, but when I tried to get it into Hugh's case it was just a little too big; the picture would have to be reduced by an inch or so. On ringing back to Henry that evening he just said 'Cut it.' What, me, cut a Henry Moore? However, I did just that, and I did not see it again until many years later when I visited Walter and Ise in their lovely house in Lincoln, Massachusetts. There it was, in the bedroom. The picture, we learned later, had crossed the Atlantic with Winston Churchill (and Hugh Weeks) on HMS *Duke of York*.

There was another delightful break from routine work. Philip Mair, a close friend of Hugh's, whose mother later became the wife of William Beveridge, who was then Master of University College, Oxford, was to be married in Oxford on Saturday 21 June 1941.

There was to be great party at the college that night, and Hugh Weeks, myself and one or two others from the Ministry of Supply travelled to Oxford in the afternoon. My diary for 21 June reads: Master's Lodge 7.30 plus rations plus Evening Dress.

It might have been before the war. There was dancing in the Great Hall, the girls in fine dresses and the men in evening clothes. I slept well after the party and came down to breakfast in the morning – a real breakfast as if in Edwardian days. On the sideboard there was fruit juice, eggs fried, eggs boiled, eggs scrambled, kidney and bacon, mushrooms – they had used our rations well. But the conversation seemed to me, in my rather sleepy condition, all academic nonsense about whether the Nazis could defeat Russia – could Russia hold out? – and what would Churchill do?

It seemed rather irrelevant, since Russia and Germany were allies and not at war with each other. Then it gradually dawned on me that something strange had happened. It certainly had. It was that morning, 22 June 1941, that Germany had attacked Russia – I had not heard the news.

And much to the relief of many, Churchill immediately broadcast at 9 o'clock saying that he was on the side of the Russians defending their homes, and that we must give them every assistance that we could.

It was not long after that that Geoffrey Dunn, who had joined up and gone into the Navy, starting on the lower deck, had a hard time of it doing the Murmansk run, which meant the worst possible weather, to the north of Russia. He was in a destroyer. I believe he did the run three times and was then given a commission. By strange and pleasant coincidence, when later he was stationed in Lowestoft he used to sail a splendid little ship, almost 26 feet long, by the name of *Kay*. Many years later we bought her, not knowing that she had once belonged to Geoffrey.

At work I was now learning how to do our job more effectively. I remember how Hugh Weeks had once told me about some American statisticians. Their figures were clear and well presented (though perhaps there were too many figures for quick understanding of the story they were designed to explain), but sometimes guns might be mixed up with howitzers, perhaps on the grounds that 'didn't they both shoot out shells of much the same size?' – regardless that each would be used for different purposes.

I at least would know such elementary facts. As far as possible I would want to find out about what I was counting and what they were for. One day early in the war Hugh, Geoffrey Crowther and I drove over to Salisbury Plain to see firing practice involving some of our new guns, including the new 25-pounder that was so urgently needed. Seeing guns in action helps to understand the supply problem. For example, all the bits and pieces that make up the breech block of a field gun, or any gun for that matter, would be listed and counted separately. It might be said that a gun could be kept in action by replacing a broken or lost small part of the breech block. Yes, but not in action, when it would be far quicker to replace the whole assembly. The controlling figure to watch, therefore, was the number of complete blocks.

I asked to see one of our air defence stations, preferably around London. I could not expect to see them in action, but perhaps I could see a demonstration simulating action. A car took me to the anti-aircraft position on Primrose Hill. They made a very realistic demonstration, loading, sighting and then even firing. It was very realistic. It certainly was – I had not heard the sirens going to announce an air raid.

Hugh Weeks's department of statistics and programmes in the Ministry of Supply did a valuable job in keeping ministers up to date on the essentials of the supply of munitions. In very many ways I was sorry to leave; the few years that I was there were often exciting and rewarding, and I carried away a great deal of valuable experience.

14
Ministry of Fuel and Power

By December 1944 we were catching up and beginning to satisfy the demands of the War Office. The 25-pound field gun was now almost becoming an infantry weapon! Now I wanted to find a job where I would be concerned with the future.

I heard of an opportunity with the Ministry of Fuel and Power in their section concerned with post-war planning. I wanted to take it up, but to get my transfer I had to be de-statisticianed – there was still a shortage of statisticians. Hugh Weeks was able to write a suitable note that did the trick without apparently denigrating me too much.

I was now to work with Roger Quirk, a very intelligent young man. His boss, Nott Bower, was Deputy Secretary. He was older and more relaxed.

Estimating the future supply of and demand for fuel was a complex and shifting problem. However, I soon found that the major use for all forms of heat was for domestic purposes, and on that I concentrated. This itself was complicated enough. There were four competing fuels, and each had its own highly efficient lobby, particularly electricity. Electric appliances, as they liked to assure us, were almost 100 per cent efficient. The fact that the national average efficiency of converting coal into electricity was then about 25 per cent was often glossed over.

The department had already considered asking the Building Research Station to put up a few houses, each of about the same size, each to be heated by different fuels – solid fuel, electricity and gas. Each would be planned to suit its particular method of heating.

At about the same time, the government had decided to build small bungalows for those bombed out of their homes. They were to be factory-produced and assembled on the site with an estimated life of ten years. The Ministry of Works, which was responsible for the programme, had already muscled in on what seemed to me to be our job, designing or selecting fuel appliances. I protested.

However, Hugh Beaver proved to be a formidable opponent and a good friend. He showed me that when a problem could be approached from different points of view there was merit in competitive research. The plan of the house might affect the method of heating, for example. The open plan would require a very different form of heating from the conventional English plan.

While at Fuel and Power I was struck by the make-up of the committees I attended. The scientists and technicians were subordinate to the administrators, who, although they had only a general understanding of the matter, took part in all the technical discussions. It was a cumbersome way of doing business.

It still seems to me that it would be much better if a high proportion of our top civil servants had a science or technical training rather than the classics and humanities, or at any rate a better balance. A few years later I read a book by Don K. Price, *The Scientific Estate*. In it he suggests that one reason why the American government is more likely to understand and to be interested in experimental ideas may be that a greater number of their top civil servants are technically or scientifically trained. He estimated that in 1960 the figure for the American service was over 40 per cent, whereas in the UK it was about 6 per cent.

Not long after I joined the Ministry, I got a new impetus when Sir Ernest Simon, later Lord Wythenshawe, was appointed as chairman of the advisory council to deal with post-war problems. The figures were by then showing that there might be a serious shortage of fuel and that it was of the greatest importance to improve the efficiency of domestic heating. He called me in. What did I know of domestic heating? Not much. What did I know of America? Nothing. So he asked me to draw up a note on why a study of American experience might be useful to Britain. I did so, in three paragraphs. He approved my note, but with a wry smile added, 'You had better make it longer.' This I did, with only a little padding, and also by dividing each paragraph into two.

This proposal was reluctantly accepted by Gwilim Lloyd George, the Minister. So there I was, in charge of an expedition to study a subject that I had only just begun to study myself, and in a country which I hardly knew at all. I insisted that I must have two experts to go with me.

I had met R.H. Rowse at the Fuel Research Station, a quiet, intelligent and well-informed man. Cecil Handisyde, an architect, was suggested. He was at the Building Research Station at Watford and had a different personality with a wry sense of humour. In addition he was great fun, and it didn't take us long to get on to good terms and make an effective team.

Nott Bower added another to the party. He well understood how important it was to record information accurately and immediately after meetings, before its significance was lost. My level in the civil service would not normally justify having a secretary travelling with us, but he managed to fix it. Irene Oberhauser, a delightful Canadian, was added to our party in Washington and travelled everywhere with us.

The work turned out to be exhausting and rewarding. We drove ourselves very hard. We were engaged on an objective study, and the experience of working with Hugh Weeks proved invaluable. It helped me to sort out unsupported opinions from those based on fact and measured knowledge.

On our way across the Atlantic in the *Queen Elizabeth*, we made plans for our work. In Washington we would meet specialists on heating and house planning and get detailed information on weather conditions throughout the country. We drew up a formidable list of searching questions. We arrived on 8 December 1944 under a steel-blue sky, and docked next to the *Queen Mary* – the two great ships together made an impressive sight.

As soon as we had landed and got through our official business, I telephoned Gropius and Breuer in Cambridge, Massachusetts, and Moholy-Nagy in Chicago. Ise said that Walter was away for the night but that I should come at once. Rowse had friends in New York, so I took Handisyde. We arrived in the dark, and slept well, very happy. Walter arrived the next morning, and as he had no key, I let him in. He was surprised to see me – it was a good meeting.

Handisyde and I spent the weekend in Lincoln and Boston, having useful talks with Gropius, who amongst other things told us that we should go to Seattle and Portland, Oregon, where weather conditions were comparable with England. He also told us about a novel plan for storing the heat generated from off-peak electric power overnight. From the Gropius's house Handisyde escaped for a while and started researching on his own. He went out for a walk, chose a house at random, knocked on the door and asked about their heating methods. Weeks later he told me that it wasn't entirely a diplomatic success. The house was occupied by a Polish family and he hadn't understood a word. All the same, we used Handisyde's methods of door-knocking and gained useful results.

Next, we all three went to Washington, where we spent nine days on our desk research. We found to our surprise that one or two American officials were a little cool towards us; we soon found out why. Some time before our visit the Ministry of Works had sent distinguished architects to buy American pre-fabs for the bombed-out in London. Instead of making quick decisions, perhaps asking for one or two minor changes, the pair had asked for alterations to the basic plans. These changes could only cause much delay, and Americans whom we met and who knew of the need for rehousing found the whole business very difficult to understand.

When they understood that we had nothing to do with any other British mission, they were most willing and helpful. The Federal Housing Authority was roughly the equivalent to our Ministry of Housing, dealing with the local authorities. The Federal Housing Administration was different. It dealt with private houses. The FHA would provide a guarantee for a mortgage for up to almost 100 per cent of the value of a house, on two conditions: there must be competitive tenders; and materials and methods of building, including equipment must be subject to regulations laid down by the Bureau of Standards. Water and heating appliances must stand up to a certain test-bench efficiency. Firms thus had an interest in designing for efficiency at low cost. This approach impressed me.

One member of the FHA staff, Robert K. Thulman, was especially helpful, and became a firm friend. He not only knew his field very well, but he knew the whole country, and he also had a sense of humour which greatly appealed to me. He told us in great detail what and who we should see, and who not to see, and indeed where to find excellent cracked crab. He also gave us some useful advice on how to travel, which is still worth following in those places where it is possible. He advised against too much air travel. He was in favour of sleeping cars on trains because they were less tiring and saved time. I also found that a Pullman berth was a very relaxing place to work.

Apart from our many official introductions, I found that I had another way of making interesting contacts. I would ring up those who worked with Molly at the Harvard Pyschology Clinic. At first they wouldn't know who I was, but then the penny dropped. 'Oh, you're Molly's husband – come and see us at once.' Molly had certainly made a mark, and I basked in much reflected glory.

Once we had finished our desk work, which proved worth every minute of the nine days we had spent on it, we set off on our travels. Our first stop was Chicago, where we arrived just before Christmas, and were taken in hand by Moholy-Nagy. He took us to an Eggnog party, and afterwards on a visit to the Institute of Design, the new 'Bauhaus in Chicago'.

Next day Moholy took us to Sears Roebuck, the mail order firm. I was again struck by the stress on testing. Sears told us that they tested all fuel-burning appliances before they would advertise them in their famous catalogue. We also saw the testing of other goods, including furniture. Moholy insisted that we should see their 'fucking machine'; it was, of course, a simple device for testing bed springs.

We went on to Seattle and Portland in the Northwest, where the climate is almost as temperate as it is in England, but we found that their heating methods were very like what we had found elsewhere in America, with open-plan houses heated from a central source. The methods developed for severe climates seem to work well in temperate ones. However, the Americans had not solved all their problems, as we were to find. From Portland we went on to St Louis, where the manager of our hotel told us that the laundry bills had been cut thanks to new local anti-smog laws that controlled the kind of coal that could be burnt in central heating furnaces. 'Why,' he said, 'now I only have to change my shirt twice before lunch.'

We visited a typical middle-class house. There was an open fireplace in the main room, but although it was cold outside and the house was pleasantly warm, the fire wasn't lit. We asked if they liked having an open fire – 'Sure, we wouldn't be without it.' We asked when they had last used it. They couldn't remember. Then the husband said, 'Was it when we had that party for Aunt Sussy?' 'Why did you have it then?' we asked. 'Oh, to help keep the room nicely ventilated.'

Later, while in Pittsburg, we visited New Kensington, a wartime development designed by Gropius and Breuer as temporary housing for factory workers. Two hundred and fifty dwellings were scattered on a steeply sloping site. They had taken full advantage of the slope to let the sun in, and the living-rooms had long windows on the south side. The value of winter sun for space heating through large glass windows was demonstrated on many occasions during our tour. Even when there was heavy snow around and the outside temperature was low, the heating system would often be turned off.

We used this idea in our house at Blythburgh many years later. The south windows let in the low sun and provide a sensible amount of heat even in an English winter.

I was interested in solar heating, but up to the time of our visit this had not been much developed in the USA, except at the Massachusetts Institute of Technology. I believed there was an opportunity to develop appliances for solar energy, either for use in Britain or for export. This idea proved to be very premature indeed as far as industry was concerned, but it did come in useful at Blythburgh. We had a swimming pool built, with a primitive solar heater of our own design. It consists of black corrugated iron sheets behind glass. When the thermostat signals sufficient heat in the sky, the pumps start drawing water from the pool, letting it trickle down over the iron, and so back into the pool. In winter the temperature rise through the heater is maybe two or three degrees Fahrenheit, and in summer we often get a heat rise of between seven and ten degrees.

We were now nearing the end of our stay. There were loose ends to tidy up. Handisyde went back to Boston and Rowse back to New York, and I went south to see how they dealt with heating and cooling in the warmer parts of their remarkable country. I took the opportunity to break my journey at Ashville, North Carolina, to visit Ati Gropius, Walter's daughter. There I met Joseph Albers of the Bauhaus. This nearly wrecked my schedule. When I went to catch my train to Charleston, I was told that it was thirty-six hours late! Several passengers were very agitated but eventually a special train was produced. It consisted of a huge engine and two coaches. I had just settled down comfortably when my neighbour, a pleasant young man who proved to be a salesman of 'suspenders' (braces), told me we were in the wrong carriage. 'Doesn't this go to Charleston then?' I asked. 'There is no time to argue, come quickly,' he said. I picked up my belongings and went to the next carriage, which was crowded, managed to find a seat, and off we went. I soon saw the point. We whites were all crowded together. In the carriage where I had been there was a nice family, father, mother and two children. They were black, and they travelled very comfortably in the almost empty carriage.

In Charleston I saw two housing estates, one for whites and one for blacks. The houses for blacks were just like those for whites, though maybe a little bit smaller. Some had combined water-heater and cooker – rather like our back boilers in England.

Later I was introduced to a newspaper editor who was described to me as a radical. I was just beginning to feel at home and started talking in the way that I thought he might expect, but caught myself just in time. Radical in Charleston means something very different – what today we might call a right-wing racist. Nevertheless he was charming, kind and courteous.

I was to meet Southern courtesy again later in the day. I was standing in the sun, thinking how lovely it all was and wondering where I should stay the night, when a large car drew up and asked if I needed a lift. I told the driver I was wondering where to stay. He said, 'Well, come and stay the night with me and the wife.' When he saw that I was hesitating he said, 'Don't worry, you can pay if you insist.'

When we all met again in New York, we still had several people to see. We were shown some excellent work, but sometimes at different universities we found research comparisons of various heating methods strangely divergent. At one place we would be shown quite convincingly how much better warm air heating was than any other form; and then at another it would be demonstrated just as convincingly that some other form of heating was markedly superior. When we found out where the money for the research was coming from, the explanation became clear.

On our way to Montreal to fly home, I had one more demonstration of the open fire as a cooling machine. I dined at Toronto with some friends of Elliot Jaques, a colleague of Molly's. They were most hospitable. The snow was almost two feet deep, and when I had taken off my heavy coat my host said, 'Now let's stir up the fire.'

There was a wide, open grate just smouldering. As soon as the fire was blazing, I could hear his central heating system starting up full blast. Of course, all the lovely warm air it was producing was being sucked up the chimney.

In spite of these experiences, we have an open fire in our living-room at Blythburgh. It does not cool the room or cause draughts, because it is provided with its own separate air supply from the outside. All the same it is a real effort for me to remember that lighting the fire will indeed make us warmer.

We had now finished collecting information. I think it was Darwin who said, 'First observation, then recording and finally reflection leading to deduction.' We had observed and recorded and were already reflecting and beginning to formulate our conclusions. Handisyde, who remained in first-rate form, had already been dictating a first draft. This draft turned out to be almost the complete job. I cannot speak sufficiently highly of the work he did. Our report was published by HMSO, and can be consulted by anyone who is seriously interested in the working part of our tour. Even now, after nearly forty years, it is relevant.

15
Bratt Colbran

The time I spent at the Ministry of Supply was a hard but interesting grind. Hugh Weeks's incisive mind was a great experience, and to follow that with the Ministry of Fuel and Power, looking ahead to post-war problems, was in many ways for me a more fulfilling experience, especially the visit to the USA and Canada which I have already described.

This visit and the published report which followed probably persuaded Lawrence Bratt to offer me a job in his firm, Bratt Colbran. They made traditional fireplaces, well designed and efficient as far as a coal fire can be efficient. They also made gas fires which had become a major part of their business, and because of that had become a part of the Radiation Group.

Going to Bratt Colbran after my two previous jobs, where an objective approach was really the only thing that mattered, was difficult, and I found it hard to cope with. The whole experience was strange to me.

At the two ministries I worked in, your position was known, and it was chiefly merit that would earn promotion; but there seemed to be other factors in the new job. A kind of bluff and bombastic superiority was needed. Family and the stake in the business was also a great help. I seemed to have none of the right qualifications. In this atmosphere, I lost some of the self-confidence I had built up in the war years.

My skills and ideas seemed to fit in no better than my background. When I tried putting forward an organized system of production forecasting that could be related to sales, it was just thought of as academic nonsense; there was no backing from either Lawrence Bratt or his brother Eric, and nothing came of it. I also tried to encourage the firm to go for export, and take advantage of a government scheme that would give a licence for extra metal and materials in short supply for firms undertaking export. However, Bratt Colbran rather frowned on it, I think because if a Labour government proposed it, it must be wrong. I had not yet learned to work with men of this kind.

There was one exception: the chairman of Radiation itself was all-powerful, and therefore relaxed and easy. It was through his support that I was able to do at least one potentially useful job; but I don't think the firm took much advantage of it.

It was my second, successful, attempt to get Bob Thulman invited to this country. Bob had been outstandingly helpful during our visit to America, and towards the end of our visit I decided to try to get my Ministry to invite Bob to London. His experience and advice would, I believed, be invaluable.

I decided to telephone London. My call through to Roger Quirk came quickly, but first there was an American voice reminding me that I must be careful what I said as the enemy might be listening. Then came an English voice which added, 'And don't forget the Americans may be listening too!'

I found, of course, that I was unlikely to get a quick decision, and back in London I found that the chances were small; there was little precedent for using foreign consultants. When I found myself in Bratt Colbran I wondered if private business would live up to its slogan and show some enterprise. It would be no bad thing if Radiation and Bratt Colbran could get Bob as a consultant for a few weeks and also offer him to the Ministry, as well as to the DSIR and local authorities.

I had talked about my idea with Lawrence Bratt, who seemed to agree, but he dithered about a decision. By the time the cable arrived from Bob saying that he had fixed everything with his Ministry, I still had not got official agreement at my end.

Lawrence Bratt was not well. I knew that Eric, his brother, would wrangle and advise no action, so I left word for him saying that I was going to drive over to see Lawrence, who lived near High Wycombe. As soon as I had gone, Eric telephoned a warning to Lawrence, who told him to stop me. Eric gave chase, but could not catch me.

This little drama did at least provoke Lawrence into telling me why things had been dragging on so. He did not have the authority to make the decision himself; the authority had to come from the chairman of Radiation. Very well, I would put the matter to the chairman. Consternation! In the end, though, Lawrence gave me a note, and off I went to Birmingham. The great man had not heard of the idea; but he liked it. 'Go ahead, young man, and fix it.' It was a small education in power politics.

So Bob did, at length, come over, and he gave us a lot of good suggestions, but they needed a great deal of pushing through. There seemed few in the group who were prepared to do any pushing and I did not think

I would be able to recruit the chairman again: so when the offer came from Herman Lebus I was more than ready to move.

16
The Russells, Herman Lebus and the design problem

When Gordon Russell was asked by J.J.Mallon of Toynbee Hall to speak to East End housewives, he told them that Utility furniture – the very plain, basic furniture which was the only sort permitted to be made during the war – was of high quality in materials and construction. A large dame in the audience asked, in a fine Cockney accent, 'What about the Utility beds?' Gordon again described how well they were designed, of fine material and well made. The large dame called out, 'Now look here, Mr Russell, my daughter is like me, ample she is, and so is her husband. He has been away two years, and next month he will have a few days' leave – now, Mr Russell, will them beds take it?'

Gordon loved telling that story.

He was a fine craftsman, especially in wood and stone, making individual pieces of furniture. He could speak and write well with enthusiasm and with convincing arguments for honesty in designing for production. This facility served well when he was director of the Council of Industrial Design. He had a powerful influence on many industries.

In 1926 Gordon changed the name of his family firm from Russell and Sons to Gordon Russell Ltd. Hitherto the name had been associated with 'craft', and now the plan was to produce well-designed furniture in quantity as well as quality. Dick, just down from the Architectural Association, was put in charge of the drawing office.

Dick was different from Gordon. He had the same attitude to quality and skill, but he designed for large-scale production including, subsequently, the Murphy Radio cabinets.

Herman Lebus met Gordon on the Utility Furniture Committee and was so impressed with his ideas that it subsequently smoothed the way for Dick, Gordon's brother.

When I joined Harris Lebus at the end of 1946, the Lebus factory, including the office, covered some thirty acres at Tottenham Hale.

I was full of hope. Herman had agreed to the appointment of Dick Russell and gave me every encouragement. Soon after I joined, Herman was not too well and went to America – a far sadder development than I then realized.

The Board consisted of Herman, his brother Louis, L.S.Lebus, and Herman's two sons, Anthony and Oliver. There was also Cuthbert Greig, Alec Jessop, Claude Symonds and myself. We all met at lunch – Herman at one end of the table and Louis at the other. I felt that I was regarded as something of a curiosity.

Greig was busy turning the partnership into a public company and arranging for its floating on the market. The firm's success had been built on low-priced, well-made cabinet furniture. Jessop had been brought in to start upholstery on a comparable scale. He was a small, tough man with strong opinions and had run a successful upholstery business. He gave me support through to the end and was sorry when I left.

The sales force were a fine group of good-looking, well-spoken men. They made many calls in the day, they seemed to be more order collectors than salesmen. They kept their eyes open for changes in retail preference and in fashion.

The competence of the technical managers was of a high order. They took instructions from the Board. They gave me every help without comment. There were two scientists – Dr Lane concerned with polish, and Dr Douglas available to be called on. He was precise and somewhat pedantic, but very helpful to me.

My first encounter with the senior technical staff was when I called a meeting to discuss a different form of construction. I proposed that the front vertical structure of a wardrobe might be of thin curved plywood, rather than the normal solid uprights. They took the suggestion at its face value without question. What about cost? This was quickly solved: I would have a cost at once. It came surprisingly fast.

Their system consisted of a library with drawings and costs of each item used in the construction, from the smallest item to each sub-assembly. When a new model was introduced, the maximum number of existing bits and pieces would be used. As design changes were usually superficial, this was easy. My proposal was not so difficult to deal with: there was little more to estimate than the two curved uprights. It was an efficient, well-managed library. I was always given the most helpful assistance, but never more than technical advice, never an opinion on whether it was a good idea or not.

Soon after joining Lebus I asked the sales department what they knew of the views and requirements of their customers. They talked of trade terms and discounts, quick deliveries, new fashions in door handles, colour and possible demand for sideboards with a waterfall front. They were thinking of the retailer and the showroom, whereas I was thinking of the housewife's requirements and the changing ways of living of the income groups most likely to be included in our price levels.

The Lebus problem was to design furniture that would meet the requirements of their customer, the retailer. But why should that be different from the retailer's customer? There was certainly a problem to be solved, and when some of Dick's designs had been made, what was it that led the salesmen to believe that the retailer would not like them? There must be a good reason. The opportunity to try and find out the reason came later.

While I believed that public taste after the war was changing, I had no evidence. To test the market, Dick and I visited a number of pre-fabs to talk with the young housewives. Apart from somewhat glamorous dressing tables which they admired, they liked the simple Utility sideboards and cupboards. Many asked why it was so difficult to get such furniture, why did the retailers prefer the more gaudy kind?

What other evidence could we get?

An opinion survey might provide guidance. I knew Dr Harry Durant and his work; his Gallup Polls had a high reputation. Herbert Morrison's 'Britain Can Make It' exhibition was still on. There was a passage through the furniture section. On one side was good conventional upholstered furniture, large and somewhat square; on the other side and immediately facing it was furniture designed by Ernest Race – an elegant easy chair on aluminium legs.

Durant placed interviewers in the gangway between these two chairs and asked the opinions and preference of passers-by, and as far as possible selecting those from the lower income groups. I was surprised when the preference for Race furniture was in the order of 30 per cent, since I had feared a lower figure.

I also found from Lebus statistics that before the war they had produced a range of bedroom furniture in limed oak. It had been designed to get into the 1935 Royal Academy exhibition 'British Art in Industry' (not to be confused with the Dorland Hall exhibition). It was surprising to find what a high proportion of Lebus sales was in that range. They were not aware of its significance.

My plan was that as soon as the Utility regulations ended and there was freedom to design as we liked, we should be ready to provide for a small proportion of our work capacity for one or two of Dick's designs. For Lebus to introduce such furniture at comparable prices to other Lebus furniture would be an event in the trade and would need hardly any extra publicity. If and when Dick's range caught on, we would be ready to increase production rapidly. Next year there would be another new design from Dick.

A number of Dick's designs were made for Herman Lebus to see on his return from the States, but he was a changed man. He ignored the evidence I produced, consulted the sales representatives, and the proposed policy was dropped. Meanwhile there were other proposals. Why not fitted furniture that could be sold through retailers? We found that among both council houses and small houses built by speculators, there was a high proportion with a chimney breast and the variation in distance between it and the wall was very small. To fit a built-in cupboard without damage to the walls, we devised a frame supported by a toggle joint, spanning the wall and the chimney breast with a tolerance of an inch or two; on it would hang shelves and doors. The experiment was successful and could carry a considerable weight of clothing. Herman was not interested. Perhaps I did not sell it properly, but I still don't think it was a crazy idea. There is now a large market for built-in units.

Then there was school furniture. The statistics showed that school population numbers were increasing and there was a building programme to match. That was 1947–8.

Dick designed tables for juniors. They had three equal sides and one long one so that when placed together they became a hexagon. They could also be put together to make as long a table as there was space available. Hertford took them up immediately and they were still in use in those schools in 1981.

Dick also designed a school desk. Working out a small production line for the desk was particularly interesting. In the firm was a young man, Mike Turpin, who worked well with Dick. The design kept closely to the requirements laid down by the Ministry of Education. We found that the new lightweight desk could be made at low cost. Dick also designed a school chair for small children, in close collaboration with Dr Douglas. The design was developed round a method of production in such a way that one man could assemble and complete the chair with the use of a simple jig from parts cut to size from the mill and the method could be expanded.

But Lebus were not chair makers and that was that. Who might make the chair in large quantities? Dick and I went down to see Lucien Ercolani in High Wycombe. Our talk hadn't been going on long when he suggested we should go and have tea on the lawn at his house. I wanted to do business; instead of tea he came on to the lawn carrying a large glass jar (it seemed at least two feet long) with ice, a bottle of brandy and bottles of champagne. I had great difficulty in keeping to business before drinking the champagne spliced with cognac. Nothing came of our meeting.

About that time Alex Clegg, Chief Education Officer of the West Riding, heard that I was at Lebus and came to see me at Tottenham. He did not like the Lebus products, but when I showed him what Dick Russell was doing for us he thought we might be able to work together.

He then told me they were converting the great country houses in the West Riding of Yorkshire, to be used as teachers' training colleges. How to convert them for living accommodation was the problem. Great high rooms divided into cubicles from floor to ceiling would make for a claustrophobic atmosphere, and lightweight partitions would not be sound-proof.

Dick suggested that the scale of the high rooms could be preserved with low partitions about six feet high, designed to provide for the storage needs of students. He pointed out that sound from one space to another is not so disturbing when it is known that there is no attempt to stop it. Many years later the same thinking emerged as the open-plan office.

Clegg's problem was that he had a buyer who kept to the regulation requiring that only the lowest tender must be accepted, leaving little or no control by Clegg. To get round that problem we evolved a different form of contract. Instead of asking manufacturers to give us a price for furniture designed by the County Architect's Department, the new contract called on manufacturers to propose a solution to the problem as well as quoting the cost, i.e. a clear brief.

Dick's design was excellent. The fine scale of the great rooms was preserved, sufficient storage was provided; the sliding doors saved space. Fixing in place was made easy and the design was also suitable for Lebus production methods. We got the order. Yet soon after that Herman Lebus decided not to go any further with the school furniture market.

The great plans for Dick and domestic furniture had been dropped. School furniture had been dropped. There was now no place for me in the firm.

Why was there such a difference of opinion between the so-called experts, the critics of design, and the manufacturers who produced for the bulk of the population? It was not just a matter of taste; the manufacturers were also uninterested in evidence about users' tastes and needs. Guided purely by the salesmen, the industry celebrated the end of the Utility scheme by piling glamour on glamour – gorgeous cocktail cabinets and amazing dressing-tables. It was said that the public liked these designs, but perhaps the reason for making them had more to do with being one up on the next retailer than with trying to find out the needs of the public.

In 1951 I was invited to give a paper to the RSA, thanks to John Gloag. It gave me the opportunity to try and find a reason for this dichotomy and perhaps a solution, and to bring reason to the discussion.

As the furniture designed in England during the seventeenth and

60. Delegates to the CIAM conference at Bridgwater in 1947. Top row, l. to r., includes Neumann (7), Richards (12). Second row, Cadbury-Brown (1), Shepheard (2), De Syllas (3), the author (14). Third row, Morton Shand (2), Martin (4), Goldfinger (5), Fry (11), Coates (12). Fourth row, Le Corbusier (1), Speight (3), Pidgeon (8), Sert (9), Giedion (10), Drew (11), van Eesteren (12), de Silva (13), Gropius (14)

61. Minette de Silva and Le Corbusier at Bridgwater. I am on the far right of the picture

eighteenth centuries was generally considered to be of a high standard, I took it as a basis. What were the social and economic conditions in those times and how did they compare with the twentieth century? From the estimates made by both Gregory King in 1688 and Patrick Colquhoun in 1815, some 80 per cent of the population were vagabonds, peasants and those with smallholdings. According to Cole and Postgate in *The Common People 1746–1946*, at least three-quarters of the income of the bulk of the population would be required for food, fuel, rent and clothing, leaving hardly anything for sickness and practically nothing for furniture.

About 20 per cent of the population in the seventeenth and eighteenth centuries consisted of the nobility or well-to-do, who lived in well-equipped houses. The bulk of the population had little more than a trestle table, a slatted wooden bed, a straw mattress and perhaps some form of chest or box.

The prosperous 20 per cent could afford to buy furniture, and if they made a mistake, they could have another piece made. Their furniture would often be designed by their architects and made by the local cabinet-maker. There would be a three-way discussion between the patron, the architect and the cabinet-maker.

The cabinet-maker attained a fame which outgrew this kind of marketing. Thomas Chippendale the younger opened a shop in 1821, first in the Haymarket in London and then in Jermyn Street, where he could show his furniture – not unlike the professional cabinet-makers of Copenhagen (Snedkemister). Still the cabinet-maker was in direct touch with his final customer.

This does not, of course, guarantee any particular standard of taste. The late Nikolaus Pevsner in his little book *High Victorian Design* points out that as the Industrial Revolution got going it was clear that the 'patrons' of 1850 were very different from the patrons of 1800.

The new rich had little education and no leisure, and these two deficiencies, writes Pevsner, 'explain nearly all that is aesthetically distressing about 1851' (the year of the Great Exhibition).

Pevsner continues: 'The appreciation of aesthetic values in architecture and design, or proportions, textiles, harmonies of colour, requires training and time. This cannot be expected in one whose mind is occupied with machine and counting house. Thus effects were bound to become louder and more obvious.'

It was furniture designed under these influences that became the prototypes of the furniture made for and offered for sale to the growing population that was beginning to afford furniture. The old culture had little influence. As the industrial world grew bigger and uglier, design offered a kind of escapism. The late Victorian novelist Ouida put her finger on this aspect of the matter when describing a most ornate clock. 'It did not look at all like what it was', she wrote, and meant it as praise.

The same process of industrialization which had caused such a radical change in taste had also revolutionized the structure of the trade. Furniture was now bought from retail shops, not from the cabinet-maker, who was now a manufacturer making more than he could sell from his own works. There was no longer any personal contact between the manufacturer and his final customer – just the situation I found in Tottenham.

Adam Smith in his *Wealth of Nations* pointed out that all goods have two values, value in use and value in exchange. The retailer is not only concerned with selling useful furniture; he is a tradesman and requires from the manufacturer not only useful furniture but something else as well. The furniture must show up well in his shop; it must look 'exciting' and different. Exchange value is not necessarily the same as use value.

For most users, even today, there is no such thing as exchange value. The bulk of the population buy furniture once or perhaps twice in a lifetime. They are therefore inexperienced buyers, and have no opportunity to make a mistake and buy again. They must learn to like what they have, as Dick Russell and I found when visiting housewives in the pre-fabs.

This argument suggests that the Design Council policy of having a selection committee made up of 'superior' people to make selections of what they considered good design was not enough. It seemed to me, that it would be better if the Council, in addition to giving examples of what critics thought was good design, could have provided an opportunity for people to choose, make a mistake and choose again; and so in a sense simulate the conditions prevailing for the rich in the eighteenth century.

Some time later I proposed such a scheme to the Furniture Development Council, and it was not far from being accepted; after all, it would stimulate an interest in furniture. There were some 350 schools that had for their Domestic Science class a couple of rooms set aside; one room was equipped as a kitchen, the other as a sitting-room. The idea was that the industry should provide a pool of furniture from which students could themselves choose, and this would be put in the sitting-room for, say, six months. Then there would be another opportunity to choose again, and what is more, mums came to tea parties, so they too would be involved.

The furniture in the pool would be selected by manufacturers as well as some pieces chosen by a selection committee of the Council of Industrial Design. Most of the members of the FDC accepted the scheme but, surprisingly, the opposition came from the educationalists, who did not like the idea of a free selection that included the kind of furniture usually found in retail shops. They wanted only those pieces which had been approved by the experts. I wanted free and genuine choice. It was a striking reminder that in education, the 'best' can be the enemy of the good.

Although we were little aware of it at first, new influences were at work. Furniture manufacturers started advertising direct to the public, bridging the gap between maker and user in the rapidly growing household magazines, and later in the Sunday supplements. Some were selling furniture by mail order, which required new techniques in design and manufacture. For a year or two at the furniture exhibition the public was now admitted, but not to the trade section. The difference in design standards in the two sections was startling.

Meanwhile the furniture for schools, colleges and the new universities was designed by architects and professional designers. Their work was also seen increasingly on television. Tastes have been changing, and so have selling methods. It is ironic to reflect that Terence Conran, who left Bryanston just as I joined the FDC, has now built a furniture retailing business with high standards of design into a huge public company. Lebus, the giant of the industry at that time, is now dead.

17
The Furniture Development Council

In the annual report of 1956, under the heading 'Summary of the Council's Services', Sir David Waley, the chairman, wrote a story of how a firm could benefit from the services of the Furniture Development Council. A firm could have installed the Council's Produce Cost System and might have discovered that they were making a good profit on articles A, B and C, but an unsuspected loss on D. They could have improved their method of purchasing and issuing stores and thus added to their available working capital. They could have increased their profits not only by ceasing to make the article on which a loss was being incurred, but also by obtaining advice from the Research Department on means of economizing on the use of timber and getting the best results from the use of chipboard and selecting the most appropriate adhesives. They could, further, have added to the well-being of employees and to profits by improving the layout of the factory and adopting more effective working methods, and by hearing from the Technical Information Service about the newest machinery and equipment. Finally, they could have combined profit with pleasure by spending a few days at the Council's conferences on management problems and on marketing and in taking part in visits to Germany and Finland organized by the Council. Then, at the end of the year, they could compare the various ratios (overheads to turnover, profits to capital employed, value added per operative, etc.) in their own factory with the corresponding figures of some of their competitors under the Council's 'Comparative Cost Scheme'.

That is not a bad list of achievements for a brand new body, seven years after its foundation, and the orderly way it was all set out is a nice example of the beautiful precision of David Waley's mind. This was of inestimable help to me in the running of the FDC. However, the story was not a smooth one of an orderly mind with a somewhat disorderly one co-operating in creating new services. It was a long struggle, and the story of how it all came about, and why the industry subsequently destroyed the body that had done all these things, though it kept many of the services, starts during the war.

There was only one thought at the start of the 1939 war – how to survive. When in 1944 the war was moving in our favour, the Churchill government set up a Cabinet Committee of Reconstruction. One idea which emerged was the establishment of development boards; the members would include government, unions and employers. They were modelled on Raymond Street's pre-war Cotton Board, and not unlike R.A. Butler's industrial charters. The government was drafting a Bill.

The furniture industry also had similar ideas and had set up a post-war reconstruction committee, with Herman Lebus in the chair. They also proposed a committee of both sides of industry with government officials. All members were to be appointed by the Minister and would act on their own personal responsibility – a big jump in ideas from before the war.

In February 1943, they discussed their plans with Sir Kenneth Lee of the Board of Trade. In August, the Furniture Committee held a two-day conference. Groups were set up to deal with the supply of timber, with labour and entry of new firms (a vexed question amongst some) – ideas not unlike the restrictions made by the old medieval guilds, the forerunners of the great City Companies of today. Quality was a special problem and their first report stated: 'Unless steps are taken to get a minimum standard of quality, certain producers are likely to flood the market with attractive looking but, in fact, junk furniture, which in our opinion should not be allowed to be offered for sale in any circumstances.'

Before the war, it would be thought that private enterprise and competition would solve all such problems. These old assumptions were now being questioned.

On 26 July 1945, Churchill lost the election, and Clement Attlee became Prime Minister of a Labour government. Instead of development boards, he set up working parties in various consumer industries. Their terms of reference were to make their own proposals aimed at raising efficiency in the national interest. They were to consist of employers, unions and independents, and a neutral chairman appointed by the Minister.

The method of appointment was significant. The Minister asked the trade bodies to send a list of those of their members who could be trusted to represent their views. The Minister would then select the members. They would be responsible to him, and free to participate as individuals, rather than as delegates of their trade bodies.

A month after the Cabinet decision to go ahead with the working parties, Sir Stafford Cripps met the Joint Industrial Council of the Furniture Industry and told them of his plan. The Council was an agency concerned with wages and conditions of labour, but it was then the only joint body in the industry. The manufacturers were lukewarm but, largely under the influence of Herman Lebus, they gave support. The unions did so too, and the Furniture Working Party was appointed in October 1945.

I was delighted when Sir Stafford Cripps invited me to be an independent member of the Furniture Working Party; Lawrence Bratt, my employer at that time, had no objection. The chain that probably led to that invitation and subsequently to one of the most interesting, frustrating and rewarding experiences of my life, started with Hugh Weeks.

When I was working for Weeks at the Ministry of Supply (see Chapter 13) I met Leonard Tregoning, whose family had an old redundant steel mill in South Wales. He said why not convert it to make Isokon furniture? The plan was put to the Board of Trade. Hugh Dalton, then president, wrote that it should be given every support. The president no doubt knew about Isokon through his wife, Ruth, who was a devotee of modern design. This may account for my name being on the Board of Trade files; so that although the mill project fell through (the Army requisitioned it), the proposal changed my life.

I found the working party terms of reference an obstacle. They were limited to domestic furniture made of wood. I protested that a vital and imaginative industry might well use other materials, and what about furniture for hotels and schools? To meet a part of my objection, a Design Sub-Group was to be formed which would be permitted to refer to the use of alternative materials. With this loophole there would be less restriction on our discussions and I was very glad to accept.

At the first meeting I found to my surprise that the Board of Trade had decided in advance that I should be chairman of the Design Sub-Group, with Gordon Russell as one of the members. We interviewed various bodies and individuals. Among the latter was a splendid Cockney manufacturer who told us that we need not worry a bit about design.

In one year you would put a piece of plastic decoration in one position and next year in another – nothing to it! Sometimes we heard that there was a fashion for waterfall fronts and many other important developments.

Such experiences made me keener than ever to find some way that would help us to start with fresh minds – away from war and pre-war ideas. A visit abroad was proposed, preferably to a country not involved in war. Sweden was suggested, but in the trade that would not be popular, for Swedish furniture was regarded as too mannered and any ideas we might bring back would be suspect. Instead we chose Switzerland. Our team included H.T.Cutler (of the High Wycombe Technical College), Gordon Russell and W.Welsford (from the furniture section of the Co-ops).

I knew the Swiss historian Dr Siegfried Giedion. He lived in Zurich and was an admirer of Walter Gropius. To get off to a good start, I telephoned Giedion and asked if he would meet us for dinner on our first night and, so that we could hear of efficient production of well-designed furniture and developments in education and training, bring one or two men who had advanced ideas and sound practical experience.

The dinner party went off well. They helped to plan our visits, we saw a lot, good efficient production, good conventional schools of furniture and also the Kunstgewerbeschule in Zurich.

This was an eye-opener. The head of the school was Johannes Itten, who had been a master at the Bauhaus under Walter Gropius. It was in fine modern buildings, with well-equipped workshops and modern machines. Johannes Itten was a man of wide intellectual, technical and aesthetic perceptions; he had been given great freedom by his governors and gave freedom for the students. He insisted that students should be confronted with art and technology together. We came back convinced that much of the high quality of Swiss production was due to that policy. Art expanded their ideas, and technology kept their feet on the ground.

I had learnt from my visit to America for the Ministry of Fuel and Power the importance of getting experiences down on paper as quickly as possible, otherwise they evaporate. Equally, we must get the basis of our report before we left for home and were back in our separate jobs. Gordon Russell had a facility for putting arguments in a persuasive way without too much ruffling up of those with other views, so it was easily decided that he was the best member of the team to draft the report.

But how to make him do it? What a game it was! Gordon had great strength and stamina, and enjoyed the delights of Swiss cookery and wine. It was not until the last night that he said he was tired, and would go to bed and make a draft. I ordered a good dinner and a bottle of wine to be sent to his room. After supper I went up to see him and found nothing done! On looking under the bed I found a second bottle – also empty – and lots of pieces of paper scattered about. It was the report! I took it up and put it into some sort of order. It was a good first draft which we were able to agree to. Our report was welcomed by the other members, and much of it was used in the report to the Minister.

The education chapter, where the ideas of Walter Gropius at the Bauhaus, Moholy-Nagy's Institute of Design in Chicago, the work of Gregor Paulsson in Sweden as well as the Kunstgewerbeschule were well reported, still seems to me important and valuable; but on rereading the design chapter, I find parts somewhat pretentious. We wrote 'There is such a thing as a standard of good design', but we did not define the standard to any great extent and we seemed to imply that those who had studied the subject were the superior few who knew what's what. This was not helpful – but reflected an attitude which was to do much harm to the work of the Development Council a few years later.

The employers in the working party remained above all interested in the problem of quality. They expressed fears that when Utility ended there would be competition from unscrupulous firms, and urged that the final report should include what they had written earlier. They added that before the war even reputable firms, under the strong pressure that prevailed at that time, were reluctantly driven to lower the quality of their goods – an astonishing confession!

The first proposal was for a British Standards Institution specification of construction, similar to Utility but with a variation licence. This would involve vetting by a BSI Committee consisting of independent experts and one or two from the industry. This would take time, and manufacturers would be reluctant to disclose new ideas to possible competitors.

Fortunately I remembered that the Federal Housing Administration guaranteed loans for housing and their equipment on condition of certain standards of quality *and performance*. Why not a test of performance for furniture? I had no idea if or how it could be done, but if it could, a manufacturer would then be free to design without restriction.

Herman Lebus and Jock Shanley saw the point at once, and they carried the rest of the working party; a recommendation to that effect was included in our report published in August 1946. Another significant recommendation was for a continuing body, similar to the working party.

Towards the end of the working party, Herman Lebus took me to lunch at the Savoy. He told me he was forming a public company, and asked if I would join the Board, in charge of the development of the product. Then he hesitated and looking at me asked, 'You're not a Jew, are you?' He seemed relieved when I told him I had not that privilege.

I started work just after Christmas 1946. In the previous chapter there is a brief account of some of the highlights of that experience. After nearly three years I had failed to make an impact and resigned. They treated me well and I departed with a year's salary.

Meanwhile the Labour party bill proposing development councils was before Parliament. The Tory opposition was against it, but when several of their own members spoke strongly in favour, they withdrew their opposition and the Bill went through as an agreed measure.

The government then, as they were bound to do, asked the views of the British Furniture Manufacturers and the National Union of Furniture Trades Operatives. In April 1948 the unions gave their support, and in September the BFM gave theirs, and so the Furniture Development Council was established on 1 January 1949.

While still in the States, after my resignation from Lebus, I had a telegram from Sir David Waley, who had been appointed chairman of the council, inviting me to become the director. The council's cable was most welcome, but they offered the minimum figure recommended in the working party report. I wanted a job, and this sounded the right one for me. I believed that if all went well it would be suitably recognized. My optimism as far as salary was concerned was hardly justified.

The Council had been provided with temporary accommodation in Cadogan Square, and Malcolm Fry had been appointed acting secretary. The most urgent job was to start collecting the levy and find a permanent office.

The terms of reference for the Development Council were much the same as for the working party. Now it became clear why we were restricted to domestic furniture and excluded furniture for other purposes, such as hotels and schools. There were trade associations for each of these groups, with their chairmen, their councils and paid secretaries. Few of them wanted to combine with each other or to come under the FDC umbrella.

Estimates of expenditure were made and the rate of levy was based on 1948 turnover, and fixed at thirty shillings on the first £1,000 of the firm's turnover, and five shillings per £1,000 on the remainder. This would be about one-fortieth of one per cent of the industry's turnover. In later years the levy for small firms was reduced further.

Searching for office accommodation was made easy. During the war, my brother's firm had been scattered, and when they found permanent accommodation we took one of their smaller offices. It was in an extension to the Adelphi Terrace but included the ground floor of the house where the Adam brothers themselves had lived.

The furniture for the council room was donated by the Scottish Furniture Manufacturers. Their designer was Basil Spence. It was elegant, but the chairs found it difficult to deal with one or two of the larger members of the Council.

Fry had kept comprehensive minutes. I was delighted to read his account of the second meeting on 13 January 1949. They were just as concerned about the dangers of shoddy furniture as were the members of the working party, and Herman Lebus had proposed a standard based on performance testing rather than on specification.

Waley had asked me, while in America, to find out what I could about performance testing. So when I joined on 11 April 1949, I told him what I had seen. As a result a sub-committee was appointed with me as chairman with instructions to get on with the research.

By May, Robin Darwin offered temporary premises in the Royal College of Art, next door to the Imperial College of Science. An advisory panel was formed that included David Pye and R.D.Russell from the Royal College and Dr Hugh Ford from Imperial College, a good start in bringing together art and science, but it was forty years before a course for designers was put on by Imperial College and the Royal College together.

By the end of the year, research had started, and in December our new research officer, Jan Seddon, gave his first report. He did it well and gave the Council sufficient confidence to call for expanding research.

Here was the opportunity that I had hoped for. A research committee of the Council was formed with one or two from the BFM.

Max Nicholson, whom I had known well in the 1930s while working on PEP, was with Herbert Morrison, Lord President of the Council. Max told me that Morrison, well aware of Britain's backwardness in industrial research, was to give greater support to the Department of Scientific and Industrial Research, and encourage the development of Co-operative Research Associations.

I met C.A.Spencer of the Department. He told me their policy was to encourage co-operative research associations; they would offer a proportion of the cost. However, the Department would on no account support a trade association. Research into testing methods only was not enough, and the director must be a scientist. My qualification of having a degree in engineering and economics was not good enough.

Then Waley met Spencer. Waley, coming from the Treasury, didn't like public money being handed over with, he thought, insufficient strings and said so. He and Spencer did not get on well. In spite of these problems, Spencer soon understood that we were not a trade association, that this old craft industry needed a wet nurse to get the baby nurtured and weaned, and that research into performance testing was one way that would lead to basic research. I was even recognized as an embryo Director of Research.

A research association, Spencer insisted, should concentrate on basic research and technical information. When we were introducing courses on costing, methods study and overseas visits, he preferred the Development Council to do such jobs. This was to suit us as well, since we found we could make a margin over cost for some of these activities and pass it on to the Research Committee, and earn further support from the Department.

During the discussion on ways to prevent shoddy furniture, a member said that if nothing was done quickly the industry would be faced with endless cut-throat competition. Waley murmured that he did not know the difference between competition and cut-throat competition. Waley's logic and dry humour was beyond some and caused him to be unpopular – he would often catch me out in the same way.

There was another occasion that puzzled Charles Lakin from the BFM. After a furniture meeting in Birmingham, Waley was travelling back by train, and so was Charles, who, on seeing Waley getting into a second-class compartment, said that the Chairman of the Development Council (which Charles so much disliked) should travel first class. Waley replied that he did not think he should spend the Council's money like that. Charles insisted and took Waley into his first-class compartment and had to pay Waley's supplement.

Towards the end of the first year we took on a young Cambridge graduate, Rafi Husain, to start a statistical service. It was well received by the Council and became a regular feature, well illustrated by charts and diagrams. Husain was with us for some time and then joined the Cabinet Statistical Department on the National Economic Development Council.

We had also sent a party of men off the bench to take foremanship courses and report back on their value. They found them useful and the Council allocated a small fund to sponsor and encourage firms to do likewise.

The Council wanted to find a way to show young workers coming into the industry for the first time, that they were joining a community with many different facets and they would not be bench hands in any old industry.

The Army Bureau of Current Affairs (ABCA) produced a fortnightly publication, and had a facility for producing easily read diagrams. Molly knew something of ABCA. She had been invited to write an article on 'Rumour', which was published on 16 January 1943. She is described as

'Dr R.Pritchard who did two years research on the subject of rumour at the Psychological Clinic of Harvard University 1940–2'. It is a splendid article and I wish she had written more; she is good at it and writes clearly and precisely. Whether it is true that she spent two years on this subject alone is doubtful, but she knew her subject well.

The moving spirit at ABCA was Boris Ford, later Professor of Education at Bristol University. He and Dennis Young (a furniture designer), using many of the ABCA methods of communication, produced a fascinating publication called *You and Your Industry*.

One member of the Council, James Cuthbert Greig, was very worried. He liked the scheme but said he had heard that Boris Ford was very left-wing, might even be a Communist, and it was dangerous to work with him. Greig was always looking for hidden dangers and Reds under the bed.

I never got to the bottom of the wicked Boris (perhaps the name was Russian?). I found him most helpful, constructive and imaginative; I never knew about his politics.

In the early days of the Council, I was invited to speak at a bi-annual conference of the National Union of Furniture Trade Operatives at Grantley Hall. I was given a generous welcome, but I was without experience and my speech was poor. Afterwards, while I was having a mug of beer, an elderly Yorkshire worker came up and with a charming welcoming smile said, 'Eh, lad, that was a bloody awful speech thou madst,' and then fell into happy conversation.

Two years later when speaking at their next conference, he came again saying much the same, but added, 'But not so bloody awful as the last one.' I was making progress.

On another occasion I did better, and instead of talking about the FDC and the two sides working together, I told them about the research work and its practical application – that was particularly appreciated.

In our second year we ran a conference on scientific thinking in business. It was attended by twelve executives, sixteen foremen and thirty journeymen. Mixing the grades, instead of inhibiting, added to the quality of the discussion.

The next conference was held in the College of Aeronautics at Cranfield. It had a Department of Economics and Production, including Methods Engineering. Again we invited all in the industry regardless of their jobs. They were to come as individuals to discuss their problems freely. As at Grantley Hall, the facilities provided were excellent.

Professor Connolly, the head of the Methods Engineering Department, said that one defect in British industry was a lack of disciplined thinking; too often we were even proud of muddling through. Too often in the past, said Connolly, timing of work was used only for fixing bonus rates regardless of how the work was done, just an inducement to work faster. Method study, on the other hand, was concerned with how to do a job more efficiently; it analysed the problems in great detail and that required measurement, both linear and time.

Vaughan Radford, chairman and managing director of Stag Furniture, showed how to reduce work in the assembly of a drawer. It was a convincing practical demonstration of Connolly's description of method study.

A few weeks before the conference a furniture trade union meeting had condemned 'time and motion study'. Believing it was only to encourage faster work they were right to condemn it. Some of their members came to the Cranfield conference. By the end, all agreed that studying how to improve the way a job was done was one thing, and useful, and was not concerned with payment by results. For incentive schemes, frank and full consultation was essential and timing could be done only by those with proper training.

I had invited a journalist, Cyril Ramsay Jones, to attend the conference and write an independent report. He wrote a good one under the title 'Work Planning and Factory Planning', with the sub-title, 'Taking the work out of the job'. The report was well received except by one member of the Council who objected to the sub-title: it might, he said, suggest we were encouraging laziness!

The third conference was at Christ Church, Oxford, and again we had all levels together. Some of the bench hands and others protested they had been given inferior accommodation. Unlike Grantley Hall and Cranfield, staying at an Oxford college might well mean walking some way for a lavatory and bathroom.

Eric Ljung, from Sweden, gave a paper on the use of engineers in furniture factories. 'Engineer' was still rather a dirty word in the British furniture industry.

Just before one Council meeting, I had a telegram from Professor Paulsson inviting me to a conference organized by the Svenska Slojdfireningen (the Swedish equivalent of our Council of Industrial Design). The Council was consulted and immediately agreed that I should go, but Herman Lebus expressed some anxiety: the Director might get exaggerated design ideas!

The Slojdfireningen was interested in our testing work and soon did much the same.

Early in 1950 we started the Technical Information Service. We were fortunate in finding John Sykes to run it. He was first-rate in searching out information and presenting it in an easily digestible manner.

When he proposed overseas visits, I need not have urged him to avoid expensive hotels – quite the reverse. The first visit was run on such a fine shoestring, there were complaints that they were too hard worked and accommodation too spartan. His preference might well have been to camp out! These visits became a regular feature.

Research was going well when Jan Seddon had a bad attack of TB and was not able to restart for almost six months. Professor Hugh Ford came to the rescue and was most helpful.

By March 1951, we needed more space and moved to sheds in an almost disused aerodrome at Redhill, again on a short lease. We now had some 3,000 square feet, a good deal more than we had at the Royal College. Work expanded fast.

On the advice of Professor Ford, Dr Russell Hoyle, a scientist from Imperial College, was made part-time Head of Research. He was not unlike the professor and could give a clear description of what he was doing. The work on performance testing was going well and we started on more basic work. We now needed a full-time manager. Hoyle thought he had at the college the very man for the job.

Michael Merrick had an easy personality, and with Hoyle's advice on his scientific abilities, he was appointed. At the time some members of the Council complained that Merrick was not even a craftsman and knew nothing of furniture. However, the Council and the industry should be very grateful to Hoyle for bringing in Merrick, who soon became highly respected in both large and small firms.

There was now developing a most unfortunate personality clash between Dr Hoyle and Dr Douglas. Douglas was an older man with a distinguished career at Farnborough, now working at Lebus. He was the only other scientist in the industry and was perhaps a little over-sensitive. Here was potential danger. They both had strong opinions. It would not help if the only two scientists fell out.

I discussed it with Waley and found that he had already begun to wonder whether Hoyle's great qualities – of which there was no doubt – might not be submerged by the problem of personality. There must be no risk, so it was with very great regret indeed that we had to lose him. There was no doubt that he was doing a splendid job. It was fortunate that thanks to Hoyle we had Mike Merrick; he became Head of Research.

At one of the furniture exhibitions at Earls Court, the BFM offered space for a small stand to demonstrate our work. F.J.Errol, president of the Board of Trade, a large man, sat rather heavily on an experimental chair. There was a sharp crack, but fortunately it stood up well.

When the time came for a further application to the Department of Scientific and Industrial Research, the Council increased its contribution and the DSIR continued their support. The work on chair testing had been completed and cabinet furniture was on the verge of success. Many found it difficult to believe, saying that of course a test on chairs could be done but it would not be possible to devise a test for wardrobes and other cabinet furniture!

While working late at the laboratory, Merrick was alone and had what at first seemed an alarming experience. There was a strong Cockney voice on the telephone: 'I 'ear you 'ave a way to make a carcass (meaning a robe, meaning a wardrobe) rigid wiv less ply – yus?' 'Yes,' says Merrick. 'OK,' says he, 'we'll be wiv you in a jiff.' Before Merrick could say that it would take time to explain the theories and that he was just about to go home, the telephone was put down and it was not long before two large motor cars arrived. Out climbed what appeared at first to be a gang of thugs – Merrick was a bit alarmed. He tried to explain the principles, but the boss man said, 'Oh, stuff all that nonsense, let's go on wiv the job.'

Meanwhile his chaps were first measuring up the wrong 'robe' when they found the right one. They were astonished at what they found – a large wardrobe, very light and absolutely rigid. Mike could do little more than look on. Later, back in their works, they tried to copy, but since they could not or would not understand the principles they made a proper hash of it. All the same they were beginning to take notice.

Merrick had made a brief study on spray polish, and as a result it was agreed to carry out a full-scale project on the distribution of spray particles. Merrick found a highly intelligent young man to do the job, and on his recommendation we took him on. I heard that he was married and living in Hampstead. I asked him to come and see us one evening. He must have thought I was reinterviewing him. He produced a rather tatty airmail envelope. I was startled. It congratulated him most warmly on a paper he had presented to a learned society; it was signed by Albert Einstein.

He was a handsome young man from India. While with us, he did valuable work on spray polishing. It was estimated that when applied it might save the industry a million pounds a year. Basic research is the backbone of any research organization. Testing is important and provides income.

When test methods had been completed for chairs and cabinet furniture, the British Standards Institution was asked to draft a BSI standard based on a test of performance, not on a detailed specification of construction. It was to be used in their 'kite mark' scheme.

The mark was designed to assure the public that products carrying it would be of sound quality and stand up to reasonable treatment. It was intended to assist those who could not afford to buy, make a mistake and buy again, and learn from the experience. GUS (Great Universal Stores) were splendid and gave instructions that all furniture offered to their public must carry the mark. It will be remembered that such a policy was called for by manufacturers before the Council was born.

Unfortunately, some makers and retailers, such as Heals, regarded their furniture as being so superior that to give it the kite mark would be beneath their dignity. They failed to understand that a few firms that made fine-looking furniture but of shoddy manufacture would themselves claim that they too made high-quality products and that they too need not apply the mark.

By being superior they provided an alibi for the spurious. Instead of congratulating GUS on their policy, they shied away and hardened their hearts against the whole scheme. The BSI failed to provide sufficient persuasion.

The Design Council was also putting a mark on those domestic articles that, in the opinion of the members of their selection committee, were approved. Here was an opportunity to introduce an element of measured knowledge to temper their opinion. We proposed that no furniture could be approved unless it was capable of carrying the kite mark. The Design Council was reluctant. Perhaps they were under the influence of those 'superior' furniture makers who scorned the mark.

There was an occasion when we could prove our point. A well-known designer, working for a furniture maker of repute, designed a refectory table. It was up for approval by the Design Council. It had two centre legs and a stretcher rail running through and jutting out at each end – orthodox and sound. The Council was persuaded to let us put the table through the normal test procedure. It failed. The horizontal stretcher, which should have been a single length of timber, had in fact been jointed and the joints hidden in the legs. It was not what it was made out to be.

The lesson was learned, but by that time the furniture kite mark scheme was dying through lack of support from any quarter. So selection was still based on opinion. Art without science had won the day; yet taste without a basis in sound factual knowledge easily degenerates into prejudice.

The Research and Information Committee was now all but independent of the Council. More and more firms, even small ones, were using both the Technical Information Service and the Research Department.

When the BFM joined the European furniture manufacturers, I was invited to one of the their meetings. The suggestion probably came from Dr Fritz Ullman, of UMS Pastoe in Utrecht, who was already interested in our statistical work. It was not long before we were serving the association of European furniture manufacturers (UEA) with a European statistical service through the BFM. European firms were generous in allowing visits from our parties, but one or two British firms did not reciprocate. Many overseas firms, to the surprise of some in Britain, were impressed with the work of the Development Council.

Around that time I had a telephone call from the Hungarian Legation. A man speaking good English said they were interested in our research; could two furniture technicians see the work we were doing? I asked him to come and see me first, he asked if 5.30 to 6 one evening would be convenient. I told him that the staff might be gone but the door would be open – just walk in. He was a little surprised at that.

A shy, handsome, embarrassed young man arrived. He was carrying a bunch of flowers, evidently on his way to pay a call. I told him we would be glad for him to bring his two technicians on condition that, after seeing the laboratory, then in Holloway, the three of them would come to supper. At that time it was unusual for those from behind the 'Iron Curtain' to venture into private homes in England.

They were duly impressed with what they saw, and I then drove them to Hampstead. We had drinks in our flat before going down to the Isobar for supper. I asked the young man what was the normal toast in Hungary. 'Prosit' said he. I told him in England we often said 'Cheerio' but that sometimes on special occasions mine was 'Damnation'.

It was at the time when Bulganin and Khrushchev came in a battleship to visit England. I apologized for the fact that people were calling them Bulge and Crush, not very dignified for such important visitors, and proposed drinking their health. The young man from the Legation turned to me with a wicked grin and quietly said, 'Damnation'!

After dinner, back in our flat, I asked what was meant by socialist realism when considering design. One of the technicians said slowly in broken English and with a mischievous expression; 'The trouble with us poor Hungarians is that we don't really understand what socialist realism really is.'

The laboratory under Mike Merrick was doing first-rate work, and in 1953 he had taken on a young Polish research worker, T. Kotas. He soon produced a theoretical paper on the factors affecting rigidity of cabinet furniture, for which he was awarded an M.Sc.

In the foreword to the published report, the scientist Sir Edward Appleton wrote that, hitherto, development had been by empirical methods rather than science, and now the work of Mr Kotas had shown there were basic principles that could be applied in various ways.

I made the mistake of letting him read his theoretical paper to a group of furniture people, in the lecture theatre of the Royal Society of Arts. There was a large audience, including chairmen, managing directors and designers, most of whom had been trained in furniture schools and colleges. Anyone with a smattering of elementary science could have grasped what Kotas was getting at, but as no one could it was regarded as rubbish. It was a dreadful meeting.

At the end, a keen supporter of the Council and its work told me he thought Kotas was not only incomprehensible, but that what he said was nonsense and that the meeting would do great harm. He was persuaded to send a wardrobe and come to the laboratory. He came, he saw, then he was impressed, but could not understand the reason why.

When we produced small models that could be handled, the Kotas principles were regarded almost as miraculous and were much admired by those who handled them; but they could not understand elementary science, they could only copy our examples. They were unable to use the principles for further innovation as Sir Edward Appleton had hoped.

Instead of the RSA meeting, I should have arranged for Kotas to give his theoretical dissertation to an audience of scientists, engineers and a few furniture men, then later have the RSA meeting with a large furniture audience at which the models would be passed round.

In spite of the awful meeting at the RSA, medium, larger and some small firms were more and more using the FDC service and also making voluntary additional contributions to the Research Committee which earned further grants from DSIR. This included £5,000 from GUS. Many firms outside the industry were doing the same, among them Aero Research, Courtaulds, Dunlop and ICI.

Periodically the Board of Trade were required to ask the Council, the unions, the BFM and all firms in the industry if they wished the Council to have a further term of life. The first review was in 1953. Members of the Council unanimously said yes, the unions separately said yes, but the BFM said no.

At first the decision by the Department was to be based on a vote from each firm, whether they employed two, three, or a hundred or more; but when we showed the Minister (a Tory) that many firms employing a substantial proportion of employment were those using the Council Research and Technical Services he decided to give it another term.

When they found the Minister was in favour of continuing the Council, the BFM withdrew their objection, provided that in future they would not send a list of names from which the Minister could choose, only the number to fill vacancies, and that they should be office-holders or potentially so. Unfortunately the Minister agreed.

Gradually this had the effect that the BFM members on the Council, although nominally responsible to the Minister, were in fact acting as delegates from the BFM. From that moment the quality of discussion at the Council faded away; but the momentum of work was such that it went on much as before.

Waley and I were now discussing how and when to launch the research committee as a fully fledged research association. The discussions began, and were well under way when, in 1957, David Waley resigned and Sir Lawrence Merriam (of BX Plastics) took his place. Here was another coincidence. My family had known the Merriams some time before 1914. Lawrence Merriam's personality and experience of industrial research gave great help to the industry. Waley, however, had been a tower of strength, giving wise and friendly advice and helping to prevent me being more stupid that need be.

By the time the Research Association was launched in its new premises in Stevenage, I was wondering when I should retire. I was already near retiring age anyway: should it be early so that my successor could move into the new building, or should I stay until we were properly settled in? The castrated Council, with the employer members acting as delegates rather than trusted representatives, had taken the joy out of the job. No longer were they interested in trying new ideas – they were far from looking in front of themselves to a new dispensation. I decided to retire early.

There was now success all round – of a kind. The BFM and the unions had joined with the Council to fulfil the promise Waley and I had made, and a fully fledged research association was born. The three bodies worked together to draft a constitution for the Furniture Industry's Research Association. We were now able to include all the technical services of the Council, such as costing and methods study which the DSIR had at first preferred to be under the FDC.

The BFM were glad to have destroyed the Council. The Council had the satisfaction of having established a research station and other new services, but now there was no agency to continue looking ahead for new ways to increase the prosperity of all in the industry in the national interest.

The Development Council had looked to the future, set up a series of activities that had proved useful and had not been there before. Why, then, did the Manufacturers' Federation want to get rid of it? There was a real reason, quite apart from normal prejudice against change and innovation. Employers' trade associations were set up to protect the interests of their members, to negotiate with other trades, with government and with the representatives of their workers. They also believed they were the body to act on behalf of the industry as a whole. Any intrusion, they believed, would weaken their power.

This was precisely the fear expressed by Sir Norman Kipping, director general of the Federation of British Industries, in 1946. He assumed that the employers' federations should be the mouthpiece of an industry. He had not yet realized that the workers were more and more regarding themselves as one part of an industry as well as members of a trade union, and that the union might well wish to join as an equal partner with the employers when, for example, making representation to a government.

Sir Norman Kipping's fear was, therefore, understandable: since, in their terms of reference, development councils were to be the mouthpiece of an industry, they could, indeed, usurp power from both management and unions. The unions had no such fear, believing they could deal with each problem themselves; it was the management side that had anxiety.

Any organization, however well run, needs a jolt from time to time, a jolt to shake itself out of itself and to think anew. Successful businesses sometimes run out of steam and become self-satisfied; they fail to notice the changes taking place and come a cropper. This applies to any organization, and I dare say to a trade association as well.

It was perhaps a good idea to set up agencies designed to give a jolt and look ahead, particularly in those industries whose constitution depends on one vote for each firm regardless of size, and where a high proportion of the total membership is made up of small firms who, by their nature, are often not so interested in new ideas. They can out-vote expenditure on various services of the kind that FDC was promoting. Such a constitution inhibits new ideas.

Lord Nathan, in his inaugural address to the RSA on 3 November 1976, entitled 'Innovation, Secrecy and Competition', dealt with one aspect of this problem.

He described how John Kempe of Flanders, who was a weaver of woollen cloth, was being prevented by the great guilds from practising and teaching his 'mystery'. King Edward III realized that John Kempe's 'mystery' was of advantage to the country, so on 23 July 1331 he overruled the great guilds, and the Letters Patent granted by the king stated: 'We take the same John, his men, servants and apprentices aforesaid and his chattel whatsoever as our special protection and defence . . .'! He certainly provided a jolt.

The guilds have now become the great City Companies and are no longer restrictive. Could they provide a jolt machine, aimed to keep an industry on its toes and prevent it from slipping back into mediocrity?

One great City Company, the Grocers Company, provided funds and encouragement so that a local school in a small town was changed into a great public school – a school that became the first to have a scientist as headmaster, who had new teaching ideas. The Grocers Company gave him strong support through many difficult periods.

Perhaps the Worshipful Company of Furniture Makers could give a lead and find a way so that it was almost obligatory for all, or almost all, in the industry to support, according to their size, a 'Think Tank'.

It would need a small staff charged with the duty of looking in front of itself, ready to promote new ideas aimed at keeping the industry on its toes, vital and forward-looking. I suppose I am advocating something very like a development council.

This may already have been in the minds of those who drafted the objects of the Worshipful Company of Furniture Makers. They are remarkably similar to the terms of reference for the Development Council. Amongst the duties, the Worshipful Company is charged not only to foster the ancient craft of furniture-making, but to encourage technical knowledge, to advance the standard of design, to direct the design of furniture to the benefit of the community, and to arrange the granting of scholarships and prizes to foster these aims.

Perhaps the Worshipful Company of Furniture Makers would implement these, and other objectives not yet thought of.

Postscript

After my retirement, FIRA continued under the direction of Geoffrey Macmillan, but owing to continuing ill-health he retired in 1969. The industry was then fortunate indeed in finding a successor. Donald Heughan was appointed and the choice could not have been better. Under his direction FIRA expanded, providing a highly efficient service to an increasing number of firms; but in 1982 the government were required to seek the opinion of the industry on the continuation of the levy. They did so by a questionnaire asking firms if they wished the levy to continue, yes or no. The Department accepted the results of the questionnaire without considering the opinions of those firms representing the bulk of employment in the industry.

Donald Heughan with great energy and determination took that in his stride, the FIRA continues maintaining a highly competent staff providing a first-rate service. The industry owes a very great debt to Donald Heughan.

18
GKN

My association with Guest, Keen and Nettlefolds was short and, I am afraid, GKN got little out of it. Working with Tom Emmerson and later with Jack Lowndes was relaxing and objective, but I did not find it so easy with those in middle and top management. It seemed to me that the management was too concerned with making money in the short run. Thinking ahead seemed expensive and academic; being useful to the community was idealistic and airy-fairy, but anyway, was it not good for all if business was run profitably? Of course the final product should be profitable. But top designers do not design their products only to make money, but to satisfy a need with a little something extra.

I met Dr Tom Emmerson at a conference concerned with industry and research, when he was in charge of the GKN laboratory and technical services. At the conference he was chairman of a group; he was splendid at keeping discussion to the point. I got on well with him, and I invited him to see the Furniture Development Council laboratory in Dalmeny Avenue in London. He came to visit one day in July 1962 and his comments were useful and to the point. Later, when I was just about to resign from my job at the FDC, or perhaps I had already done so, he invited me to be a consultant to GKN in some form or other.

This all seemed rather vague to me, so I asked to be given a job description. 'Jack Pritchard' was Tom's reply. Emmerson felt that an outsider with very different experience might be useful if for no other purpose than give a jolt to accepted ideas. Besides giving a small and welcome addition to a meagre pension, the job gave me the opportunity to use my experience in a new direction.

One useful achievement was to introduce Jack Lowndes, GKN's technical information man, to Herbert Spencer. Jack had been impressed with the FDC technical bulletin and wanted to improve GKN's regular bulletin. I had told him that we had employed Spencer as a typographic designer at the FDC. Our experience, on a much smaller and simpler scale, had shown that a typographer understood the problem of using the printed word as a means of efficient communication. Jack Lowndes, very much concerned with doing a good job, saw the point quickly, and I believe the results were good.

Another task that did produce results was to deal with finding an architect to design an extension for the laboratory at Wolverhampton. It was to cost some half a million pounds. The request came over the telephone

one morning: could I, who knew so many architects, suggest someone? I wanted time, but Tom said there was hardly any time so I recommended Yorke, Rosenberg and Mardall. They were modern in the best sense and thoroughly professional.

Rosenberg brought a team to see us. We met at dinner in Wolverhampton and the project was discussed. They asked many searching questions and went away to sleep on it, and then, much to the surprise of GKN, they turned it down. I don't think GKN had met that kind of architect before or expected that an architect would turn down a half-million-pound job from a great firm like GKN. It was a good experience for them.

The architect who eventually got the job was sent on the recommendation of Yorke, Rosenberg and Mardall, and he didn't do a bad job at all. He was chosen because he insisted on a detailed brief, including discussions with heads of sections.

When I first started work with GKN Tom took me to the head office in Kingsway and showed me where I could get typing services. Very foolishly, I was slow at getting down to real work that might have been constructive and did not take advantage of what GKN was offering me. Perhaps it might have been better if Tom had decided on some project to work on and first discussed it in great detail. What an opportunity there was there, and I missed it!

One job I very much wanted to follow through was the design of office equipment. This was seldom tackled in a fundamental way. I had had some very interesting correspondence on design during the war with the Reconstruction Secretariat of the Cabinet Office and also with Walter Gropius. This discussion was on an objective level, with very different attitudes from those of the GKN managers for Sankey Sheldon Office Furniture. Their view was that, after all, the office desk was an office desk; it needed only minor changes to meet current fashions. Why a high design?

Sankey Sheldon were making steel office furniture and they were concerned with selling steel. Sankey's manager did the designing himself and saw no need for a consultant designer. But work that was done on a desk was surely changing fast due to the invention and production of new machines. Would it be possible to begin to make guesses of future office procedures? Would it loosen our minds to watch the changes that had taken place during the last hundred years and help us to project future possibilities? Without strong support for my ideas it was difficult to get through to top management, but I should have been more forceful.

Many years before, towards the end of 1931, I was working at Venesta and much involved with the Design and Industries Association (DIA).

Some of us wanted to make the DIA think ahead and plan their activities, to concentrate on one thing at a time. The president of the DIA was Frank Pick and he gave us much encouragement.

The result was a quarterly journal with an editorial board of John Gloag, W.F.Crittal, Max Fry and myself. We decided that a theme for the first issue would be 'the office', with Max as editor for that issue. At that time my brother, Fleetwood, needed new furniture, and instead of making guesses, the two of us studied his basic needs and then designed and made the furniture especially for those needs. It was an amateur job, but valuable experience.

GKN were promoting a number of educational activities and scholarships. David Beck, who was doing freelance work for Jack Lowndes and myself, thought it would be a good plan to channel all their educational projects together and start what might be called a GKN Foundation. It could attract one or two educationalists and professors and could become a highly respected body promoting educational facilities that would look to the future. Nothing came of it.

Almost at the end of my association with the company, I got to know Monty Berman, who had been in charge of Form International. Both Monty and Form International seemed to be doing quite well, but when new capital was required to meet his rapid expansion it was not forthcoming from America, where the company had been set up. Art Metal, part of the Form International/Parker Knoll Group, was the chief competitor of Sankey Sheldon (a part of GKN), and one standard method of dealing with competition is to buy it up. I suggested to GKN that they should do this, but at the same time take the chance to acquire Form International with its excellent design team. This would give a jolt to Sankey. But unfortunately GKN was only interested in Art Metal and this fell through anyway.

Finally there was solar heating. While Molly was at Harvard she saw a small experimental house at MIT. It was February and the house was deep in snow. The temperature inside the house was 70 degrees Fahrenheit and the tap water was too hot to hold your hand under. The house was heated only by the sun. This was the work of Professor Hotle and Dr Maria Telkus. Solar heating was in normal use in Israel, and Hotle and Telkus had shown in their world survey that many other areas could use solar heating just as efficiently as the Israelis. There could have been a good export market for standard solar equipment, but GKN didn't take up my suggestion – perhaps it was too airy-fairy.

BLYTHBURGH

19
The Broads and the Martham Yard

When our boys were three or four we wanted to take them sailing. My Uncle Clifford had a bungalow at Horning where when going upstream, the river Bure turns more to the west and slightly south. It was next to a boat yard owned by Dick Southgate. My uncle suggested we should hire half-deckers from Dick, and stay in the cottage. This we did. Dick Southgate taught us a lot about sailing on the river: how to sail against the stream amongst the trees and when there was hardly a breath of air.

The Broads were badly affected by the war. All boats had to be taken out of the water: many were left in the open on the banks where they dried out, their timbers would shrink and their seams would open up; only the best boats would find space in a shed. One night Dick's Yard, where a few boats were stored, caught fire and all the boats were destroyed. Dick, who was getting old then, died soon after of a broken heart. We believed his son would have liked to continue in his father's business, and we thought we might buy the Yard for him. Unfortunately the big boat-building companies were after it, and we were not able to compete with them on the price they offered.

The great shame was that Dick's son should not even have one of his father's boats. I pleaded with the group who were buying the yard to do something for the boy, and in the end they said we could have any one half-decker, provided it was taken immediately. That was on a cold Saturday evening in December! Chris, Dick's foreman, Molly and I would like to have taken *Mischief* or *Nimble Nell*, both very good boats, but they were too far from the water for us to take immediately. So we took *Betty* – quite a good little ship and she was near the water's edge.

My uncle's bungalow was on the river front next to Dick's Yard, with a dyke behind joined by smaller dykes to the river. *Betty's* timbers were dried out, so she would take in water fast – could we get her round before she sank? We managed, with a lot of bailing, hauling and paddling, to get her behind my uncle's bungalow and, some time later, when the Martham Yard was in operation, we had her put into condition.

Our negotiation to buy Dick's Yard was through an auctioneer and land agent in Wroxham, and when we failed to get it he told us of another yard for sale at Martham. Although we said we didn't really want a yard, he persuaded us to go and see it.

The Yard was at the end of a bumpy lane and consisted of a dry shed,

62. On the Broads at Thurne in *Kay*

63. Mollie Thwaites, Edward Ardizzone, Russell Hoyle and myself on the Broads in *Twenty Six*. Drawing by Ardizzone

about 35 by 40 feet, and next to it a wet shed about 38 by 18 feet wide. There was good simple equipment, including two sailing cruisers, *Merry Heart* and *Nyanza*, moored on Hickley Broad. There was also a fine half-decker, *Albatross*. We thought it would make an excellent place for holidays – camping in the sheds and sailing the boats – so we took the plunge and bought the lot for £1,100. Then there was the problem of getting the boats into proper condition – a problem soon overcome by an introduction to Jimmy Brown and his friends Durwood Wright, Frank Skoyles and Maurice Davey. They had been working in the Herbert Woods Yard making power boats for war contracts. Jimmy and his friends undertook to put our three boats into order, and it was not long before we received letters from Jimmy telling us that the work was going well. Our three boats were ready by March 1945; to put them into sailing condition had cost £160.

Two projects were now floating in our minds: one was to do with the children's holidaying, using the boat yard as a base, which was ultimately to become Theta; the other was to start a boat-building company with Jimmy Brown and his friends.

In drawing up plans for a company, we wanted Jimmy and his friends to be equal partners with us, so we put the Yard in at the price we paid, including the boats that were now in sailing condition, and we would value their tools, equipment and knowhow at the same figure and arrange the shares accordingly. By October 1945 we had drawn up the heads of agreement for a company.

Meanwhile, Harry Mansell, who before the war had been making the Isokon Long Chair and other Isokon products, introduced us to Ken Gibbs. Ken designed a boat for us. It was not a great success but good fun – 26 feet long with a beam of 6 feet and a 32-foot mast. At first we called her *Twenty Six*. She was built by Jimmy Brown and his friends. When designed she had a small cabin, but we decided that it would be more fun if we stripped her of all but essentials, so we changed her name to *Gipsy Rose Lee* and did away with the cabin superstructure – she then sailed rather better. Ken Gibbs also designed a scow for us. The brief was that it should be large enough for two children but not for an adult and a child. This was because, when an adult was in a boat with a child, it was always the adult who had the tiller; this was no way to learn sailing – sailing has to be learnt by making your own mistakes. These little craft were named Tiddlers – 10 feet long, 4 feet 6 inches wide and with a 22-foot mast with jib and main. Three were made for the Theta club, which was in its early stages of development. They were paid for by Della Harris, mother of Anthony and Edda, but in a few years the club had managed to pay her back. One of the Tiddlers was on show at Heals for Christmas 1946. They were very good fun and did teach the children quite a lot about sailing.

The Yard, under Jimmy's direction, was doing very well. It not only dealt with boat hire and repair, but also with building construction. Hardly was the ink dry on our agreement than Jimmy had bought wartime aircraft hangars. They were made of simple light girders and cost nothing more than taking them down and away. They were then sold to local farmers for agricultural sheds. The company did quite well out of them. In view of Jimmy's interest in building I proposed a small group of two or three houses in Martham. I had recently returned from the Fuel and Power mission to America and Canada and had in mind that Cecil Handyside, who was with us, should design them using, perhaps, warm-air under-floor heating. When we told Jimmy about the system, he said that pigsties were often built that way; they were very delicate animals, he said.

The Martham Boat Yard quickly developed into a fast-expanding business, largely due to Jimmy's considerable energy. By the time he died, in 1976, the yard owned over one hundred sailing boats, half-deckers and motor cruisers.

20
Blythburgh

We enjoyed living in London, especially in No. 32, Lawn Road Flats. Our flat gave us immense pleasure, greatly enhanced by Philip and Kathy Harben's Isobar. Our sailing weekends were easy to arrange: Molly worked in Cambridge on Thursdays, and on Fridays I would catch the train to Norwich and Molly and I would meet there. We would then drive up to Thurne together, where we would usually join friends for the weekend. We did this most of the year. But Thurne was hardly the place to retire to.

Finding the site in Blythburgh, in 1961, was a fortunate accident. We had already been tempted towards Blythburgh. Molly and Jeremy had spotted the two wartime pillboxes on the field near the water tower and had speculated on a house poised between them – a house with a fine view of the estuary to the north and east.

The Mill Farm was for sale with a pleasant two-storey house, somewhat Regency in character, and with about fifty acres of land. We came up and picnicked by the birch trees on the south side of the house and watched the fine expanse of water at high tide and then the mud at low water – all very tempting for Molly, who was now a dedicated bird-watcher. So, we took a big gulp and bought the whole lot, planning to sell the existing house and to build a house where we had picnicked, amongst the birch trees: a house of today and tomorrow, designed to bring in that spectacular view.

Dick and Helen Collett, who had been friends of my brother, Fleetwood, bought the Mill Farm house and are as pleased with the position as we are. We were to rent the grazing land to local farmers and preserve the meadows between the house and the estuary.

But who were to be the architects for our house? We had both been impressed with a house that my daughter (with her husband, Colin) had designed for Beatrix Tudor Hart in Fortis Green, and although they were a bit disconcerted when asked to be our architects (Colin later wrote: 'Jack and Molly knew more about architecture than was good for any client') they agreed to do it.

Molly and I tried to define our requirements, not as regards design, but to try and imagine the way we would want to live. This would be the beginning of the brief, but we did have a strong prejudice for a flat roof. A flat roof would not spoil the view of the house opposite, would settle into the landscape and would hardly be seen from the east. Indeed, it is very difficult to spot the house from the river. We had said we would like one large room with as much glass as possible to bring the wonderful outside in, and we did need a separate space for eating, preferring a working kitchen to a dining kitchen. We would like a guest room, a bunk room and perhaps a guest bathroom. Our own room and bathroom were difficult: we found it hard to describe what we wanted – we did not know. Certainly we wanted sleeping and storage accommodation and also space for a desk and bookcase. Of course it was hard for Colin and Jennifer to design, and they did well, giving us flexibility.

Many schemes were produced: an 'L' shape was tried, two blocks parallel but staggered and linked by the dining area, plans that included a courtyard, a pitched roof, etc. But somehow we always came back to the simple, rectilinear idea, and the final plan was for a basic, simple cube. A good architect is supposed to reflect his client's desires and emotions, and Jennifer and Colin's design for our house at Blythburgh has achieved this.

Jennifer had already designed pre-fab houses for the GLC and I still had an interest in the Martham Boat Yard. And so it was that our house, with its timber frame, plywood and plaster board with Western red cedar cladding, was built in a boat yard – partly assembled in the yard and brought over for erection on the site. It took nine months to complete.

The splendid fireplace in our sitting-room is an afterthought. The chimney and fireplace design is unique to Colin and gives a maximum area of warm plaster and brick. The rest is a Baxi fire which takes in fresh air from the outside (from below the floor) and does not, therefore, as so many open fires do, take the warm air from the room and send it straight up the chimney.

While the house was being built we decided to add the pavilion, on the

64. Our house at Blythburgh, Suffolk. The chimney in the living-room while under construction
65. Front view of the house, which was designed in the early 1960s by Jennifer and Colin Jones
66 and 67. View of the back of the house, with the large living-room approached from the estuary and garden

road side. Always known as the 'girls' football room', it too was designed by Jennifer and Colin and built in the Martham Yard.

We have a swimming pool, not a tiny pool but a real one. It fits, snug and almost out of sight, behind the high banks of dug-out earth. Because of my long interest in heating and my experiences in America and Canada, I had wanted to try heating a pool with solar energy — and so that is what we did and it works well throughout most of the year. The pool and its companion sauna have provided me with the most delightful luxuries.

The house has many special merits — one of which is the feeling of being relaxed and easy, which could be due to the entrance, which is not mean and narrow, and the way into the living-room, through a 'passage' we call the picture gallery.

Coming to Blythburgh starts a new chapter. First we used to visit for weekends. Then, when I had resigned from the FDC and Molly from her clinics, we spent ten days in London and ten days in Blythburgh. Gradually the ten days in Blythburgh got longer and our time in London shorter until we gave up the flat and settled, finally, in our house.

In an article in the *Guardian*, Diana Rowntree described the house in favourable terms but the heading is 'The Ideal Client'. I wonder if Colin and Jennifer would agree? They took so much trouble to give us the house we wanted and the one which we love so much.

21
Final chapter

From a midshipman in a battle cruiser to landing in Cambridge was like jumping out of a dark room into the light, with an ever-expanding view instead of a necessarily imposed discipline. Now I could do, think, and say what I liked.

At school I had been a slow starter; at Cambridge my mind was opening up fast, and that was exciting. I was surprised and delighted to get a Second in engineering and particularly a First in economics, a subject that continues to intrigue me.

Those two years gave direction to much of my life. Into them I crammed a lot. I joined the Union, arguing, debating, and tried to join three different political parties. I was welcomed by Liberals and Labour, refused by Conservatives because I had joined the others. They wanted the purest, not those who challenged the *status quo*. I was now catching new ideas on the wing, a widening experience. I attended lectures, some not listed for my exams. One series was 'The Scope of Industrial Psychology' by Philip Sargent Florence. It was rewarding; and Philip introduced me to Henry Morris. What a revelation that was! His Saturday and Sunday walks got rid of preconceived ideas, leading me instead to wonder, ask questions. With him I met friends for life.

Among them were Tom Lupton, who used his private resources always on worthwhile jobs, and Ruth, his wife, who, in spite of physical handicap, worked for those in need, for which Wallingford gave her the freedom of the town. Another friend was Henry Rée, a gentle educationalist who became a brave Resistance leader in Nazi-occupied France. Then there was Robert Shaw, a housing administrator who, despite his enthusiasm for Henry's ideas, preserved a tidy mind, and kept us on the straight and narrow; the ever-faithful Ian Philips, always ready to give support to Henry and his schemes; and the bouncing David Hardman who became Parliamentary Secretary to the Board of Education. And of course the lovely Jacquetta Hawkes, who later married J.B.Priestley. Her son, Nick Hawkes, was an early prop of the Theta Club. Her book *A Land*, with Moore illustrations, was scholarly, beautifully written and produced; much later came *In Quest of Love*, a strange delightful story, followed by the exciting biography of Mortimer Wheeler.

Henry urged that, for a worthwhile job, the greater the element of social good, the greater the satisfaction. That was so when Wells Coates solved

68. Myself in a Marcel Breuer Long Chair at Blythburgh. Beside me is the Mark 2 Penguin Donkey

Molly's brief for the Lawn Road Flats. His elegant plans for the minimum flat provided the mechanics of an easy life-style for young professionals. The Heating Report (commissioned for the Ministry of Fuel and Power, to which I refer in an earlier chapter), though it appears dryly technical, also affected everyday life, by showing how a low-cost house could be kept warm throughout the year at less cost than with the conventional spot heating so common in England; it ensured that we no longer spend the winter round the hearth. That gave me satisfaction; and so did my job at FDC, where I was working with others to make the industry more efficient.

In this chapter I raise subjects that I believe to be important – subjects which perhaps need tackling by wiser ones than me. One of these is administration and the special qualities which it demands.

Contrary to the popular belief that a professional administrator can manage anything, Henry stressed that, for anything worthwhile to be achieved, administration must be in the hands of a philosopher with an agile mind. The unimaginative ones only do what they are told.

Henry himself, by blending together a variety of public services, for example public libraries, juvenile employment, old people's clubs as well as education, invented the concept of the Village College, and half a dozen were built in his lifetime in Cambridgeshire.

Another example is Herbert Morrison, who chose Gerald Barry to run the 1951 Festival of Britain. It was run efficiently but in a creative spirit, with British whimsy thrown in. Few professional administrators would, for instance, have considered the famous Skylon designed by Powell and Moya with the engineers Samuely and Partners (of which my son Jonathan is now a partner). In the Festival of Britain, Barry's qualities of imagination were applied to project the English tradition into the future. This is just one example which I think bears out my argument that the general problems of administration need further thought.

Gerald Barry also promoted a series of papers to be given in the Guildhall. One which especially impressed me was by Alistair Cooke. His paper described how the world's population was divided unequally. The vast majority, brown and black, were predominantly destitute and starving. But these people were now, through improved communications, especially television, beginning to see how the rich whites were living and that, he predicted, might lead to disaster.

He reminded me of how the Roman Catholics were preaching against contraception to those same expanding destitute populations. I find this evil. God certainly urged us to fertilize the earth. The good gardener does that. But he carefully prevents his crops from overgrowing, so allowing the health-giving ones to survive.

Again, it was Alistair Cooke, in one of his 'Letters from America' in 1981, who emphasized another problem of particular concern to me, and of relevance to my experience at the FDC. He described how, in the 1920s the mill workers in Lancashire, who had no say in policy, watched their textile machinery being sold; as they had no other craft they now had no work. The machines went to Japan and were used to make comparable material at lower cost. How was this done?

In Britain it is relatively recent practice for the boss to work with his technicians to find improved methods to be handed over to the workers to carry out. In America it has been normal for the boss to work with his technicians but seldom with the workers. In Japan it is altogether different, for to find ways to improve efficiency the whole staff, including the workers, are involved.

At our FDC conferences on methods to improve efficiency, all levels joined together on equal terms – only a few of the more superior bosses being noticeably absent.

Many of these problems would hardly have arisen had we, in the sixteenth century, done what the philosopher Francis Bacon urged, and pursued science in the aid of mankind, setting up a truly balanced education for us all. We would now be an educated nation. France, a few hundred years later, both before and after the Revolution, established a school system that included science; Europe, and most of all Germany, followed, but the French Revolution had so alarmed the English upper classes that they, believing it had been sparked off by scientists and secularists, avoided science like the plague. The teaching of history and the classics was far safer. It was not until the 1914–18 war that the government understood how far ahead was German industrial research, and only then we in Britain set up the Department of Scientific and Industrial Research (DSIR). One of their jobs was to promote co-operative research in any industry that was prepared to have a go. The furniture industry was one.

The urge to pontificate in this last chapter is hard to resist. What I write may be half-baked; but surely that is better than not to be baked at all.

Once with Herbert Samuel I argued that the soviet election system might have merit. But Herbert pointed out that the village soviet elected a member for a soviet of a larger area and so on through several layers until the supreme soviet is reached, and it is they who appoint those in authority. The people are left far behind with no direct contact as in a parliamentary democracy. In Tzarist Russia the people had no direct influence, and when cracks appeared the system collapsed. Might not this happen in Soviet Russia? It is not unlike a drop leaking from a tap; a drop appears, it seems stable, but then suddenly collapses. This could happen in a parliamentary democracy with only two parties, whose policies are getting further and further apart, leading to catastrophe, but with more than two parties progress might be slower but there is less chance of disaster.

I have been much stimulated by the theories of my friend Richard Goodwin, Professor of Economics at the University of Siena, in his proposals for an alternative to a strict monetary policy. Writing in the spring of 1980, in the *Journal of Post-Keynesian Economics* (vol. II, no. 3), he points out that Keynes gave a clear and convincing analysis of how capitalist economies might be able to provide for full employment. Partly as a result of Keynes's influence, he says, the post-war period has been one of continuous growth and output. But since 1974–6 this trend has been broken, influenced perhaps by the oil crises and growing unemployment.

Richard Goodwin writes that John Maynard Keynes may not have envisaged the effect of too rapid a rise in wages and salaries which encouraged imports, but the introduction of an agency aimed at relating prices and earnings, similar to the agency presided over by Aubrey Jones in 1965–70, plus a Keynesian policy, would increase production and so reduce unemployment and discord.

69. Simon Loftus, on stilts, at our fiftieth wedding anniversary party at Blythburgh

Goodwin then refers to the 'Multiplier', which, as I understand it, goes like this. When a business wants to improve its methods and expand it invests. It may borrow money or use what it has in the bank. Workers will be re-employed and start spending again, unemployment pay is now avoided and, as the firm becomes profitable, it buys more material and rebuilds its capital. Since more goods go on the market there will be a tendency to reduce inflation. Such a policy could be carried out by state enterprise as well as private. The 'Multiplier' would stimulate all sections of an economy and give hope rather than creating frustration. No doubt much else must be done: we need to have a government of active compassion and one that includes thinkers and philosophers who can think ahead, using the practical ones to carry out their policy. We will then rebuild our country with imagination, looking forward, free from class distinction.

Looking back over the pattern of our life, it seems that Molly and I have been fortunate that in times of need we have been able to help both Henry Morris and Walter and Ise Gropius; many would have done the same. The thanks they gave were typical of each. The letter from Henry Morris published in Harry Rée's *Educator Extraordinary*, is so beautiful, and the one from Gropius so typical, we have decided to give them here.

Henry wrote:

> I have been thinking a great deal of what I owe to people, the debt is a big one, but I have no doubt that I owe more to you than to any other two people. The reason is quite clear, you gave me confidence, more than anybody, and consistently. Jack, more than any one man, believed in me and made it clear without display . . . you, Molly, did

the same for me. . . . The benefit in confidence and security for me over thirty-four years has been unstatable. I knew I could, without hesitation, turn up at any time at Lawn Road Flats and be welcome – welcome is not good enough a word. I mean received with affection so that one felt one mattered (a lovely feeling). Neither of you, by the way, ever made demands. I also had the subconscious assurance that when difficulties or dangers arose which I could not cope with, I could, if necessary, go to you without an apology on my lips. Well, I have told you the truth, and it is good to do so.

Not long after he wrote that letter he declined rapidly and died at Hill End, St Albans, in a room by himself. There he was, lying peacefully, his hand was hot; I kissed him on his forehead and wished him a happy crossing of the Styx into glorious oblivion.

On 17 May 1968, Chip Harkness and his wife gave a party in their home in Lexington to celebrate Gropius's eighty-fifth birthday. The cake was cut, 'Happy Birthday' sung: Gropius's reply was short and unexpected. 'Thank you,' he said; 'now fill your glasses and drink to Molly and Jack for saving our lives.' But it was really P.Morton Shand who saved their lives, by getting Max Fry to offer a partnership, and Isokon to give hospitality and promote building projects.

These and other influences would never have developed without Molly; we have such a stable loving life together, her fine efficient mind, her qualities and abilities married into mine, providing a firm base on which to think, work and act. The children at Beacon Hill School, in answering a general knowledge question, said we were a well-assorted couple. How right they were.

In finishing this last chapter, I don't think I can do better than to quote from my grandfather who, when he was about ninety-four wrote: 'In regard to religion, my views are, in the main, founded on my understanding of the works of J.S.Mill, Charles Darwin, and T.H.Huxley, and as to my conduct in life, I try to be guided by the principles of altruism coupled with the desire to create as much cheerfulness as possible.'

70. The Pritchards at the pool in Blythburgh. The family group includes our sons Jeremy, far left, and Jonathan, centre, with my daughter Jennifer, right, and her husband Colin who were the joint architects of the Blythburgh house

SELECT BIBLIOGRAPHY

Books and articles
This list does not include books already noted in references and sources

Architectural Review 1930s special issue
November 1979

Banham, Reyner
'Isokon Flats', *Architectural Review*
July 1955

Boumphrey, Geoffrey and Coates, Wells
'Modern Dwellings for Modern Needs', *The Listener*
24 May 1933

Dean, David
The Thirties: Recalling the English Architectural Scene,
RIBA Drawings Series
London: Trefoil Books, 1983

Garland, Madge
The Indecisive Decade
London: Macdonald, 1968

Hanson, Brian
'Rhapsody in black glass', interview with Raymond McGrath,
Architectural Review
July 1977

Haworth-Booth, Mark
E. McKnight Kauffer: A Designer and his Public
London: Gordon Fraser, 1979

Hughes-Stanton, Corin (ed.)
'Gropius and the making of Impington –
correspondence deposited at Newcastle University'
Design, London, February 1974

Jackson, Anthony
The Politics of Architecture
London: Architectural Press, 1970

Kostelanetz, Richard (ed.), *Moholy-Nagy*
London: Allen Lane, 1971

Lever, Jill
Architects' Designs for Furniture, RIBA Drawings Series
London: Trefoil Books, 1982

Morris, A.E.J. and Murphy, Cornelius
'Max Fry: Inspirations, friendships and achievements of a lifetime in the Modern Movement', *Building*
31 October 1975

Naylor, Gillian
'Modernism: threadbare or heroic?' *Architectural Review*
August 1977

Read, Herbert
'A Nest of Gentle Artists', *Apollo*
September 1962

Rée, Harry
Educator Extraordinary: The Life and Achievement of Henry Morris
London: Longman, 1973

Richards, J.M.
Memoirs of an Unjust Fella: An Autobiography
London: Weidenfeld & Nicolson, 1980

Rowntree, Diana
'The Ideal Client', on Jack Pritchard, *Guardian*
26 September 1963

Sharp, Dennis (ed.)
The Rationalists: Theory and Design in the Modern Movement
London: Architectural Press, 1978
(Includes an extended version of the obituary of Wells Coates by J.M. Richards first published in the *Architectural Review*, December 1958.)

Skelton, Robin (ed.)
Herbert Read: A Memorial Symposium
London: Methuen, 1970

Stamp, Gavin
'Conversation with Ernö Goldfinger', *The Thirties Society Journal*,
No. 2, 1982

Two books in preparation are especially worth noting: Professor Reginald Isaacs's life of Walter Gropius, and Terence Senter's study of Moholy-Nagy's years in England.

Exhibition catalogues

Art in Britain 1930–40 centred around Axis, Circle, Unit One
Marlborough Fine Art, London, 1965

Bauhaus
Royal Academy, London, 1964

Marcel Breuer
Monograph by Christopher Wilk accompanying exhibition
Museum of Modern Art, New York, 1981

Circle: constructive art in Britain 1934–40
Kettle's Yard Gallery, Cambridge, 1982

Wells Coates, Architect and Designer 1895–1958
Oxford Polytechnic exhibition at Museum of Modern Art, Oxford,
1979

Gropius in England
Pamphlet by David Elliott accompanying the Gropius travelling exhibition
Building Centre Trust, London, 1964

Hampstead in the Thirties: A Committed Decade
Hampstead Artists' Council exhibition at Camden Arts Centre, London, 1974
Including a commentary on Isokon by Alastair Grieve

Isokon
Hatton Gallery, University of Newcastle upon Tyne, 1980

Lubetkin and Tecton: Architecture and Social Commitment
Arts Council and University of Bristol Architecture Department, 1981

I. Moholy-Nagy
Arts Council of Great Britain exhibition at ICA, London, 1980

Alastair Morton and Edinburgh Weavers: Abstract Art and Textile Design 1935–46
Scottish National Gallery of Modern Art, 1978

A New Design for Living: Design in British Interiors 1930–51
Book, ed. Timothy Prus and David Dawson, accompanying exhibition at B2 Gallery, Wapping
London: Lane Publications, 1982

Thirties
Arts Council exhibition at Hayward Gallery, London, 1979

A Tribute to Herbert Read 1893–1968
Bradford Art Galleries exhibition at The Manor House, Ilkley, 1975

Unit One: The Modern Movement in English Architecture, Painting and Sculpture
Exhibition at New Burlington Gallery, London, 1934
Accompanying book of same title edited by Herbert Read
London: Cassell, 1934

Lectures and articles by Jack Pritchard

'The Changing Character of Furniture'
Paper given at the Royal Society of Arts and reprinted in the *Journal of the Royal Society of Arts*, No. 4867
22 February 1952

'Gropius, the Bauhaus and the Future'
Paper given at Royal Society of Arts and reprinted in the *Journal of the Royal Society of Arts*, Vol. 117
January 1969

'Lawn Road and the Thirties'
Pidgeon Audio Visual, tape PAV 795
London, World Microfilms Publications, 1980

'Must We Make the Same Mistake Twice?'
Paper given to the Design and Industries Association and reprinted in the *DIA Year Book*
1979

Index

Aalto, Alvar, 61
Akerblom, Dr, 123
Albers, Joseph, 138
Appleton, Sir Edward, 62
Army Bureau of Current Affairs, 157–8
Arnold, Graham, 50
Artists' International Association, 16
Atkinson, Edgar, 58
Atkinson, Robert, 79
Attlee, Clement, 151

Barnes, William, 99
Barry, Gerald, 62, 63, 64, 99, 180
Bassett-Lowke, 112–13
Bassingbourne Village College, 50
Bauhaus (Dessau), 57, 106, 109
Bayer, Herbert, 23
Baynes, Ken, 110
Beacon Hill School, 20, 70, 72–3
Beaver, Hugh, 134
Beck, David, 170
Belgion, Montgomery, 86
Berman, Monty, 171
Bernal, J.D., 21
Beveridge, Mrs William, 86
Blackett, Sir Harry, 63, 64, 65, 66
Blake, A.E., 65
Blythburgh, 174–8
Bossom, Alfred, 64
Bower, Nott, 134, 135
Bratt, Eric, 140, 141
Bratt, Lawrence, 140, 141, 152
Bratt Colbran, 140–50
Braun, Robert, 94
Breuer, Marcel, 17, 21, 86, 92, 97, 111–21
British Furniture Manufacturers (BFM), 155, 164, 165
British Standards Institution, kite mark scheme, 161
Brown, W.J., 86–90
Browne, Neave, 101
Bryanston School, 73–5
Building Trades Exhibition, London, 60
Bunbury, Sir Henry, 63, 64
Butler, R.A., 50

Cabinet Committee of Reconstruction, 151
Camden Borough Council, 99–100
Campion, Sir Henry, 90
Carter, Edward, 17
Casson, Hugh, 86
Cazalet, Thelma, 15, 84
Charte d'Athènes (Athens Charter), 11
Chawner, W., 38
Chermayeff, Serge, 12, 13, 91
Childe, Gordon, 90
Chippendale, Thomas, the younger, 148
Christie, Agatha, 19, 86, 97
CIAM group, 11
Clayton, Ann, 65
Clegg, Alex, 145–6
Coade, T.F., 73–4
Coates, Wells, 11, 12–13, 18, 53, 56, 60, 92; *see also* Lawn Road Flats
Collett, Dick and Helen, 174–5
Colquhoun, Patrick, 148
Conan Doyle, Sir Arthur, 38–9
Connolly, Cyril, 22
Connolly, Professor, 159
Conran, Terence, 150

Cooke, Alistair, 180, 181
Cooke, Henry, 30, 31
Cooke, Jill, 30, 31
Cooke, Sammy, 48
Craven, Ida, 27
Craven, Nellie, 27
Cripps, Sir Stafford, 152
Crowther, Geoffrey, 133
Crowther, Jim, 21
Cutler, H.T., 153

Dannat, Trevor, 22
Design Council, 162
Design and Industries Association (DIA), 80, 81, 169–70
Dickinson, George, 39
Digswell Art Trust, 50
Dobb, Maurice, 62
domestic science class furniture, 149
Dorland Hall exhibition, 80
Douglas, Dr, 143, 145, 160
Dugdale, John, 51
Dunn, Geoffrey, 117–18, 132–3
Durant, Harry, 142
Dursley-Pedersen bicycle, 129

Elliott, David, 110
Elmhirst, Leonard, 64
Embling, David, 84
Emmerson, Tom, 168
Entwistle, Clive, 112
Ercolani, Lucien, 145

Federal Housing Administration (FHA), 136–7, 154
Federal Housing Authority, 136
Feigl, Fritz, 22
Fenn, Charles, 48
Fenwick, Trevor, 39
Festival of Britain (1951), 180
Field, Marshall, 124
Fifty Years of Economic and Political Planning, 11, 67
Filipowski, Richard, 122
Fisher, Kenneth, 29
Florence, Lella Sargent, 38, 86
Florence, Philip Sargent, 15, 38, 86
flush door, 56, 57
Forbes, Hugh, 160
Forbes, Mansfield, 10
Ford, Boris, 158
Fordham, A., 45
Form International, 170
Freud, E.L., 22
Fry, Julian, 40, 41
Fry, Malcolm, 155
Fry, Maxwell, 10, 11, 14–15, 24, 57, 80, 170
Furniture Committee, 150
furniture design, 142–50
Furniture Development Council, 149, 150–67
Furniture Industry's Research Association, 165, 167–8
Furniture Working Party, 152

Gabo, Naum, 21, 22, 92
General Strike (1926), 62
Gibbs, Ken, 173
Giedion, Carola, 111
Giedion, Siegfried, 153

Glass, David, 131
Gloag, John, 54, 56, 81, 112, 122, 146, 166
Gloag, Mim, 91
Goepfert, Louise, 58, 60
Goldfinger, Ernö, 16
Goldsworthy, W., 27
Goodhart-Rendel, 79
Goodwin, Richard, 182
Gordon Clark, N.J., 65
Gordon Russell Ltd, 142–3
Gould, Michael, 86
Goulden, Gontran, 110
Granville, S.R.K., 90
Great Universal Stores (GUS), 162, 164
Greig, J.C., 158
Groag, Jacques and Jacqueline, 17, 86
Gropius, Ati, 138
Gropius, Ise, 16, 107, 110
Gropius, Walter, 11, 16, 17, 86, 96, 101–9, 181
Gropius Architectural Exhibition, 109–10
Gruenberg, E.A., 83
Guest, Keen and Nettlefolds (GKN), 168–70
Gurdjieff, G.I., 58–60

Half Hundred Dining Club, 18, 91–2
Hampden nursery school, 20
Hampstead, 9, 14, 16–18
Handisyde, Cecil, 135
Harben, Kathy, 94, 174
Harben, Philip, 18, 91, 92, 94
Hardman, David, 48, 50, 51
Harkness, Chip, 183
Harrison, Jill and Harry, 79
Hastings, H.de C., 83–4
Hawkes, Jacquetta, 48, 179
Hayward Gallery, 'Thirties' exhibition, 13, 101
Heals, 162
Henry Morris Memorial Trust, 48
Hepworth, Barbara, 14, 21, 92
Heretics, the, 38
Heughan, David, 167–8
High and Over, 84
Highpoint, Highgate, 17, 84
Hill, Polly, 86
Holman, Portia, 69
Howard, Doris, 69
Howe, Jack, 105
Hoyle, Russell, 160
Hudnut, Joseph, 127
Hughes-Stanton, Corin, 99, 100, 109–10
Hunt, H.A., 99
Husain, Rafi, 157
Huxley, Julian, 18, 21, 63, 64, 65

Impington (Cambridge Village College), 17, 47–8
Isobar, 17, 18, 19–20, 92, 94–5
Isokon, 80; Bottleship, 117; Dining Chair, 115; Gull, 117; Long Chair, 112–15; Penguin Donkey, 115–17; Pocket Bottleship, 117
Isokon Line, 115
isometric unit construction, 80
Itten, Johannes, 153

Jacobsen, Arne, 113–15
Jacques, Elliott, 139

Jeanneret, Pierre, 60
Joint Industrial Council of Furniture Industry, 152
Jones, C.R., 159
Jones, Captain, RN, 36, 75
Jones, Colin, 175–6
Jones, Jennifer, 20, 69, 86, 172–6

Kanthack, Tim, 40–1
Kapp, Edmund, 86
Kempe, John, 166
Kepes, George, 124
Keynes, John Maynard, 39, 63
King, Geoffrey, 148
Kipping, Sir Norman, 166
Kokoschka, Oskar, 22
Korn, Arthur, 17, 86
Kotas, T., 163–5
Kropotkin, Peter, 109

Lakin, Charles, 157
Lancaster, Osbert, 9, 19–20
Lane, Allen, 115
Lane, Dr, 143
Laurie, K., 40–1
Lawford, Ben, 32
Lawn Road Flats, 13, 15–16, 19, 22, 78–100
Layton, Tommy, 92
Lebus, Anthony, 143
Lebus, Herman, 142, 143, 154, 159
Lebus, L.S., 143
Lebus, Louis, 141
Lebus, Oliver, 143
Lebus factory, 142–50
Le Corbusier, 9, 11, 60, 80
Lee, Sir Kenneth, 151
Lindsay, Kenneth, 64, 65
Ljung, Eric, 159
Llewelyn, Brian, 24
Llewelyn-Davies, Richard, 99
Lloyd George, Gwilim, 135
London Zoo, new architecture, 21
Love, Dr, 55
Lowndes, Jack, 168
Lubetkin, 17, 60
Lupton, Ruth, 179
Lupton, Tom, 48, 179
Luterma, 53

MacCarthy, Fiona, 24, 101
McGrath, Raymond, 10, 12, 13
Macmillan, Geoffrey, 167
Macmillan, Margaret, 70
Madge, Charles, 90
Mair, Philip, 132
Mallon, J.J., 142
Mallowan, Max, 86
Mall Studios, 14
Mandeville, John, 131
Mansell, Harry, 112, 173
market research, 54
Marquand, Hilary, 90
MARS group, 11
Martham Yard, 171–4
Martin, Kingsley, 99
Martin, Leslie, 21
Massingham, Dorothy, 58
Maw, Graham, 91
May Committee (1931), 63
Meidner, 22

Mellor, David, 24, 101
Mendelsohn, Eric, 56
Merriam, Sir Lawrence, 165
Merrick, Michael, 160, 161
Mesens, 22
metal-plywood folding doors, 10
Meynell, Francis, 18
Ministry of Fuel and Power, 133–40
Ministry of Information, 129–33
Ministry of Supply, 130, 133
Moholy-Nagy, Lazlo, 17, 18, 21, 86, 121–7
Moholy-Nagy, Lucia, 121
Moholy-Nagy, Sibyl, 22, 111, 126
Mondrian, Piet, 22
Monsarrat, Nicholas, 86
Moore, Henry, 14, 21, 90, 95
Moore, Irina, 90
Morris, Henry, 10, 38, 44–51, 65, 98, 103, 182–3
Morrison, Herbert, 144, 156

Napier, Montague, 83
Nash, Paul, 14
Nathan, Lord, 162
National Union of Furniture Trade Operatives, 158, 159
Neal, Laurence, 64
Neap, Jack, 63
Nehru Memorial Exhibition, 110
Neill, A.S., 71
Newman, Lena, 95
Nicholson, Ben, 14, 21, 92
Nicholson, Max, 11, 64, 65; *A National Plan for Great Britain*, 62, 63, 64
Norton, Peter, 124

Orwell, George, 14
Ouida, 149

Paepeke, 124
Paimio sanatorium, 61
Paulsson, Gregor, 86, 152
Percy, Lord Eustace, 45
Perriand, Charlotte, 60
Pevsner, Nikolaus, 15, 97, 118; *High Victorian Design*, 146
Phillips, Ian, 48, 179
Pick, Frank, 81
Pinder, John, 67
Piper, Myfanwy, 21
Plymex, 55
plywood, 53–5
Political and Economic Planning (PEP), 10, 11, 62–8
Poor Man's Wine and Food Society, *see* Half Hundred Club
Postgate, Raymond, 18, 91
Potter, Jeremy, 99
Price, D.K., 135
Pritchard, Clive Fleetwood (father), 27
Pritchard, Dr Eric, 68
Pritchard, Fleetwood (brother), 27, 123
Pritchard, Jack: early years, 27–9; naval service, 34, 37; meets Molly, 37; at Cambridge, 37–41; with Michelin Tyre Company, 42–3; with *The Field*, 43; with *World Today*, 43–4; marriage, 44, 68; with Venesta, 44; designs Plymax sideboard, 56; and Venesta Flush Door, 58; visits Luterma factories, 61; in

General Strike, 62–3; and PEP, 64; sailing, 75–8, 169–72; acquires Martham Yard, 75; Lawn Road Flats, 80–98; member/chairman, Design and Industries Association, 10, 81; at Ministry of Information, 129ff; at Ministry of Supply, 131, 133; at Ministry of Fuel and Power, 134ff; visits USA, 135–40; with Bratt Colbran, 140; with Lebus, 142; joins Furniture Development Council, 150; with Furniture Working Party, 152; with GKN, 168; at Blythburgh, 174–8
Pritchard, Jeremy (son), 68ff
Pritchard, Jonathan (son), 68ff
Pritchard, Lilian (née Craven) (mother), 27
Pritchard, Maria (daughter-in-law), 95
Pritchard, May (sister), 27
Pritchard, Molly (wife), 9, 10, 20, 30–4, 44, 68, 75, 155–6
Pritchard, Nancy (sister), 27
Pullman Court, 84
Pye, David, 156

Quirk, Roger, 134, 137

Race, Ernest, 144
Radford, Vaughan, 159
Radiation Group, 140
Read, Herbert, 11, 14, 21
Rée, Harry, 48, 179, 182
Reeves, Frere, 43
refugees, in Britain, 16–18
Reid, Graham, 54, 61
Reilly, Paul, 10, 14, 96
Richards, J.M., 13, 92
Riss, Egon, 17, 115, 117
Robertson, Howard, 79
Robinson, Kenneth, 86, 101
Rowntree, Diana, 86, 96, 178
Rowntree, Kenneth, 86, 96

Rowse, R.H., 135
Russell, Bertrand, 20, 69
Russell, Dick, 142, 144
Russell, Dora, 20, 70
Russell, Gordon, 142, 152, 153–4
Russell, R.D., 156
Rutherford, Henry, 54, 123

Samuel, Herbert, 181–2
Sanderson, F.W., 29
Sankey Sheldon, 169
Sawston, 46
school furniture, 145
Sears Roebuck, 137
Seddon, Jan, 160
Sert, J.L., 11
Shand, Morton, 24, 61, 102, 183
Shanley, Jock, 154
Shaw, Robert, 177
Shepheard, Peter, 109
Sieff, Israel, 64, 66
Simmonds, Gudrun, 110
Simon, A.P., 104
Simon, Sir Ernest (later Lord Wythenshawe), 135
Slutsky, 17, 22, 92
Smith, N.W., 65
solar heating, 138, 170
Spence, Basil, 152
Spencer, C.A., 156–7
Spencer, Herbert, 118, 168
Spicer, Robert, 55, 65, 91
spray polishing, 161
Stamp, Josiah, 64
Stevenson, Dr, 50
Stokes, Adrian, 15
Strauss, Mr and Mrs George, 13, 20
Summerhill School, 71–2
Summerson, Sir John, 12, 22
Sun House, Frognal Way, 19

Sunspan Homes, 19
Svenska Slojdfireningen, 86, 159
Sykes, John, 160
Symonds, Charles, 143

Teapots, the, 38
Techplan, 10–21, 65–7
Thalman, R.K., 137, 141
Tillett, Ben, 63
Tregoning, Leonard, 152
Tudor Hart, Beatrix, 20, 69, 79
Turpin, Mike, 145

Ullman, Fritz, 163
Usherwood, Kenneth, 131
Utility furniture, 142

Van Eesteren, 11
Venesta, 53–61, 82
View on Planning (New Atlantis), 67
Village College, idea of, 45

Waggoners, the, 54
Waley, Sir David, 150, 155, 156
Walker, Gilbert, 131
Walton, Joan, 47
Ward, Montgomery, 124
wardrobes, 143, 161
Webber, Christine, 118–20
Week End Review's National Plan, 64
Weeks, Hugh, 105, 130–2, 132, 133
Weissenhof, 16
Wells, Gip, 38
Welsford, W., 153
Whiskard, G.G., 63, 64
Wood, Sinclair, 54
Worshipful Company of Furniture Makers, 167

Yorke, Rosenberg & Mardall, 169
Young, Michael, 63